In Focus Railways in the North West

Peter Hill

Left: Pacer unit No.142052 pulls away from the WCML onto the Ormskirk Line with the 17.22 ex-Preston train on 25th June, 1988. Until the late 1960's this was the principal route between Preston and Liverpool. Nowadays, InterCity services travel via Wigan and St. Helens Central, while passengers on the Ormskirk line have to change to Merseyrail services at Ormskirk.

Frontpiece: **Class 31/1 No.31196** *in very dirty Railfreight livery has been pressed into summer passenger service on the 17.07 Manchester Victoria to Southport, and is seen crossing the Leeds-Liverpool Canal at Gathurst, near Wigan, on the evening of 7th August, 1988. Many trains on the Southport route were loco-hauled during the summer of 1988 due to a shortage of Pacer and Sprinter units at Newton Heath depot in Manchester.*

Front Cover: **A Pacer unit is dwarfed by the moor and mill chimneys which surround the village of Portsmouth on the Copy Pit route.**

Back cover: **Class 90 No.90009 waits for a clear road at Preston, December 1988.**

All photographs throughout by the author.

Coorlea Publishing,
West Lodge,
Taverham Hall,
Norwich. NR8 6HU

Copyright © Coorlea Publishing 1989

All rights reserved. No part of this publication may be recorded, stored in a retrieval system, or transmitted in any form or by any means, electrical, mechanical, photocopying, recording or otherwise, without the prior written permission of the publishers.

ISBN 0 948069 09 0

Design: Ashley Butlin

Series editors: Ashley and Jenny Butlin

Typesetting: Coorlea Graphics

Printers: Haynes Cannon Ltd., Brunel Close, Wellingborough, Northants.

Acknowledgements.

My thanks are due to a number of people for their help in this project. To Father Peter Sayer for permission to photograph from St. Walburge's Church, I extend my grateful thanks. Also to Ron and Nora Martin for their guidance and help. Finally, to my wife Lilian and children Daniel, Oliver and Tom for their total understanding at all stages and to whom this book is dedicated.
Peter Hill March 1989.

Contents

Introduction	3
Liverpool and Manchester	5
Warrington, Wigan and Preston	13
The Cumbrian Coast	22
Carlisle. The Border City	26
The Settle and Carlisle	30
Trans-Pennine Routes	35
The Peak Forest	43

Introduction

Contrary to popular belief, the North West of England was at the forefront of railway development in this country. Many railway historians would have us believe that the Stockton and Darlington Railway of 1825, constructed by the famous locomotive builder George Stephenson, was to take the title "Birthplace of the Railways". But 13 years earlier, in 1812, Robert Daglish of Orrell, near Wigan, had built a locomotive of the adhesion type to work the local colliery yards, and in 1825 (the same year as the opening of the Stockton and Darlington), the County of Lancashire was granted an Act of Parliament for the construction of the Leigh and Bolton Railway, the building of which was supervised by Daglish. The largest railway project of this time, though, was the Liverpool and Manchester Railway which received Royal Assent on the 5th May, 1826, and was officially opened in front of 50,000 people on 15th September, 1830.

After the Liverpool and Manchester came an avalanche of smaller independent lines including the Warrington and Newton Railway, the Wigan Branch Railway and the Kenyon and Leigh Junction Railway, to name but a few. Eventually the Warrington and Newton Railway combined with the Wigan Branch Railway to form part of what we now know as the West Coast Main Line (WCML) between the two towns.

As they became an integral part of the Industrial Revolution, the railways gradually took over the work of the canal narrow boats and pack horses with effects which were to bring permanent change to the region's economy and social life.

It was "all quiet on the Western Front" for the next 150 years as the North Western Railways went about their daily business. It was 1955 before the area began to reel under the effects of the Modernisation Plan, and in 1962 the Beeching Plan caused havoc among the small rural branch lines as well as some main line routes. With the multiplicity of competitive routes built in the 19th Century, the railways had signed their own death warrants and began to suffer from the effects of a boom in road transport following the Second World War. In 1923 at the amalgamation there were some 20,000 route miles

Class 87 No.87025 County of Cheshire passes over the Leed-Liverpool canal at Wigan close by the redundant Westwood Power Station, which is soon to be demolished to make way for a leisure complex and marina. The locomotive is working the 07.50 Glasgow Central to Poole "The Wessex Scot", as far as Birmingham New Street, where diesel power will take over. The Leeds-Liverpool Canal opened in the late 17th Century and was made obsolete with the coming of the railways. Today, it sees pleasure crafts instead of the once familiar horse drawn, and later, steam-driven coal barges.

which were reduced to 11,000 by the early 1960's, a great and sad loss.

Looking at more recent times, the mid 60's and early 70's have seen the arrival of air conditioning and comfort on InterCity electric services from Euston to Manchester, Liverpool and Glasgow. Super sprinters are set to enhance Provincial services to the North West from South Wales, the Midlands and the North East. On the freight side there have been drastic changes too, with numerous smaller marshalling yards closing down to be replaced by Speedlink yards such as Warrington Arpley, an integral part of the BR freight network. Looking to the future, the Channel Tunnel should bring more rail opportunities to the North West for both passenger and freight operations.

This book gives an overall view of the modern day scene covering an area from Warrington in the South, to Carlisle in the North, from Liverpool in the West, to Manchester and the Trans-Pennine routes in the East. At present, North West railways are enjoying a spectacular resurgence with new stations, rolling stock and locomotives; the future must augur well for this intriguing area of British Rail.

Just one mile from the centre of Bolton, the 10.29 Kirkby to Manchester Victoria passes rural Lostock on the 14th May, 1988. The service was well patronised by Saturday shoppers on a day trip to Manchester.

Liverpool and Manchester

The birth of the Liverpool and Manchester Railway was brought about by the dire need for a reliable connection between the two towns, both of which had expanded rapidly in the late 17th and early 18th Centuries. No sooner was the raw cotton arriving in Liverpool from the United States in vast quantities than the finished products were despatched from Manchester. The Leeds to Liverpool canal linking the two towns proved inadequate for the large amount of trade which was flourishing. The initial plans for this famous railway were those of William James and Joseph Sandars, virtual unknowns in the railway world. James was a lawyer from Warwickshire and Sandars was a partner in a Liverpool Corn merchants. James had visited Northumberland where Stephenson was gaining a reputation as a locomotive builder, and by 1822 had surveyed a route which would take the line by Rainhill and over both Newton and Chat Moss. Sandars was to provide the financial backing.

Unfortunately, in 1823, James was made bankrupt and Robert Stephenson was appointed engineer, only to be dismissed two years later because of errors in his survey of the route. Enter George and John Rennie as engineers and Charles Vignoles as the route planner. Also re-enter Robert Stephenson who had by now made his reputation with the Stockton and Darlington Railway, and became the Liverpool and Manchester principal engineer. The line received Royal Assent on 5th May, 1826. As late as 1829, locomotives to work the line were still being discussed, some thinking that 'Fixed Engines' should be used, others deciding to hold an 'Improved Engine' Competition with £500 being offered for the best built locomotive. Stephenson's "Rocket" was judged the best entrant and from that moment the line's motive power had been finalised.

The official opening on 15th September, 1830, saw eight trains leaving Liverpool for Manchester, carrying more than 700 guests including the Prime Minister of the day, the Duke of Wellington. The locomotive was named "Northumbria" and was driven by George Stephenson. Unfortunately the well documented accident occurred at Parkside when William Huskisson, MP, alighted from the train and was run over by the "Rocket" as he tried to shake hands with the Prime Minister.

It was decided to continue the journey to the Liverpool Road terminus in Manchester because of the vast numbers of people waiting for the train there. Huskisson died the same evening and a marble monument still stands to his memory by the line at Parkside Junction. Regular passenger services began two days later, but the real object of the line was to carry freight and these trains began to run in December 1830.

After the building of the Liverpool and Manchester Railway many more independent lines mushroomed in the area, including the Liverpool and Bury Railway which eventually gave the Lancashire and Yorkshire Railway a route between the two counties. Lime Street Station was opened in 1836 and trains ran through to the Midlands as well as Manchester via the Grand Junction Railway. Almost immediately opposition was faced with the opening of the Chester and Birkenhead Railway. In 1846 the Liverpool, Ormskirk and Preston Railway amalgamated with the East

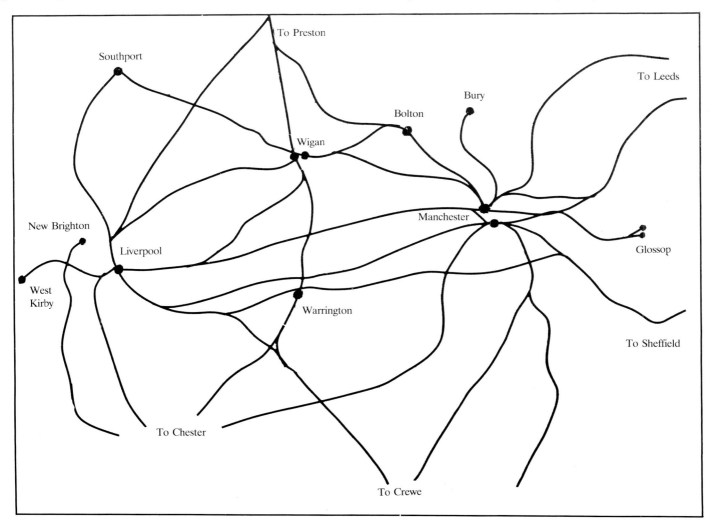

Above: Class 31/1 No.31164 trundles along the Folly Lane branch at Runcorn with the 6T65 local chemical tank trip from the ICI complex to Warrington Arpley Yard on the 20th June, 1988. This branch was electrified in the late 1960's to handle work from Willesden Yard in North London. This traffic, however, was withdrawn two years ago when Brent Council in London complained to BR about the hazardous loads of chemicals left in sidings close to residential property within the Brent Borough (which includes Willesden). Today the wires still stand but the branch is used solely by diesel traction.

Below: Class 03 No.03162, but carrying its old number D2162 and having an inscription painted on its cab side to the old Birkenhead Mollington Street MPD, is pictured on a household coal working in the heart of Birkenhead dockland on the 18th January, 1988. At the time BR had only three Class 03s on its books, the other two being 03073 and 03170, all allocated to Birkenhead North depot for dock work. These two locomotives are in BR corporate blue, whilst D2162 is in a BR green livery.

Lancashire Railway which opened a station in Liverpool to become known as Exchange, built between 1884 and 1888.

The Lancashire and Yorkshire Railway began an extensive programme of electrification at the beginning of the 20th Century with Southport coming on stream in 1904 and Ormskirk in 1913. These two lines are of course still running today under the Merseyrail banner.

The Grand Junction Railway's approach to Liverpool was still a long drawn out affair, with traffic joining the Liverpool and Manchester at Earlestown. By the time the GJR had become part of the LNWR, a bridge had been constructed to carry the line over the River Mersey at Runcorn, and Liverpool was reached via Ditton, passenger services beginning to use this route in April, 1869. The other large station in Liverpool city centre became known as Central, and was opened in 1874, run by the Cheshire Lines Committee.

One of Liverpool's most famous landmarks after the Liver building was the Overhead Railway which was the first in Britain to adopt an automatic signalling system and also provided the first escalator known in this country. The first section of line was opened in 1893 and was very well patronised, becoming known to Liverpudlians as the 'dockers umbrella'. During the Second World War the line was damaged by German bombers, but the permanent way staff soon had trains operating normally again. Passenger traffic gradually declined and the line was closed in 1956. Today there are few reminders of the LOR, the preservation movement being far less active in the late 50's. Thankfully, Power car No.3 survives at the Merseyside Museum and Trailer No.7 is preserved at Steamport Museum, Southport.

On the other hand Merseyside's underground railway system has had a far more successful career. The first public service ran in 1886 when the Prince of Wales opened the line between James Street in Liverpool and Green Lane at Tranmere on the opposite side of the Mersey (later extended to Rock Ferry). The first services were run by steam traction, the smoke causing many problems for both the travelling public and footplate crews as the trains travelled beneath the River Mersey. Electric traction replaced steam in 1903 and the system became the first in the country to oust steam from a principal rail network. Today it is the busiest commuter service outside London.

In 1977, a new underground station was opened at Moorfields to cater for the area around the former Exchange station, and in the same year a new electric service to Kirkby on the Wigan line began. A loop line was opened also in 1977 serving the Mersey and Wirral lines, with trains running clockwise to Central and back to James Street, although the deep level platforms at Lime Street and Moorfields were not open until 1978.

Today Liverpool, which once had three main line stations, has only one, namely Lime Street. Trains depart from there to destinations throughout the British Isles, and of course the original Liverpool and Manchester line still plays an important role in the BR network.

InterCity Electric traction in the form of AC electric locomotives arrived in Liverpool from Crewe on the 18th June, 1962. Until then principal express services had been in the capable hands of LMS Pacifics based at Edge Hill. In the early 50's and 60's Liverpool had many steam depots including Edge Hill, opened in the late 1800's, Speke Junction, Bank Hall, Aintree, Brunswick, and Walton-on-the-Hill. Brunswick was the first to be closed in 1961 followed by Walton in 1963, Bank Hall (1966), and Aintree (1967). Edge Hill and Speke Junction were the final steam strongholds on Merseyside, closing in 1968, just a few months before the end of steam on BR. Speke was used as a dump for withdrawn London Midland locomotives long after steam had vanished from BR metals, and Aintree is now the only depot standing, albeit in a very derelict state and painted with graffiti. A diesel servicing shed was built at Edge Hill soon after the demolition of the steam depot but this is now derelict, although part of the coaling ramp is a reminder of things past. A modern

---

Class 47/4 No. 47488 is pictured at speed approaching Parkside Junction with the 11.05 Newcastle to Liverpool Lime Street Trans-Pennine service of the 24th June, 1988. The locomotive is yards from the spot where William Huskisson, MP, was knocked down on the 15th September, 1830, as he tried to shake hands with the Prime Minister during the opening of the Manchester and Liverpool Railway. A marble monument to the MP stands along side the main line at Parkside Junction.

Class 508 Merseyrail electric unit No.508135 runs past Birkenhead North No 2 box with the 13.34 New Brighton to Liverpool Central on 11th November, 1988. In the left background can be seen the Bidston East Junction box which controls the diverging lines to West Kirby and New Brighton. Semaphore signals are very prominent in this area of the Wirral.

traction depot was built in the early 60's at Allerton, a mere stone's throw from Speke Junction, and still services electric units and locos as well as diesels and multiple units. At weekends, modern traction is also to be found stabled at Lime Street Station, and also Speke Yard (on the site of the old steam shed) rather than on Allerton depot where work today is concentrated on locomotives and units using the wheel lathe and re-fuelling facilities. The occasional diesel and electric loco also stable near Downhill Carriage sidings along with two Class 08 shunters.

Freight trains on Merseyside are mainly of the Speedlink and Freightliner variety working to and from Garston Container Terminal. Train loads are despatched each working day to such places as Willesden, Stratford, Tilbury and Crewe. Speedlink duties deal with Company trains from Aintree (Metal Box), Speke and Halewood (Ford Motor Company). The BOC plant at Ditton sends block trains to the Midlands whilst the ICI complex at Folly Lane, Runcorn, trips many loads to Warrington Arpley Yard for despatch nationwide, using the freight only line between Ditton Junction and Arpley. Class 58s also work into Garston with coal export trains from Toton.

Passenger loadings are very healthy on Merseyside, especially the London workings with the Liverpool Pullmans doing exceptionally well. Many commuters use the Merseyrail electric services travelling into the city from Birkenhead, Ormskirk and Southport. A new semi-fast service between Liverpool and Preston via Wigan was introduced at the beginning of the October 1986 timetable offering the best timings since the abandonment of the through workings from Liverpool Central via Ormskirk which ended in the late 60's.

At the beginning of the May'88 timetable, a new service between East Anglia and the North West under the 'Express' banner meant the end to Class 31 haulage on the Sheffield-Liverpool workings, the new trains being worked by Class 156 Sprinters based at Norwich. Problems have been encountered with overcrowding on this route since the Sprinters run as two-car formations unlike the loco-hauled trains which ran with five carriages. Amends are being made, however, with some Sprinter units being extended to four carriages.

When the Liverpool and Manchester Railway first arrived in Manchester it was not greeted with open arms by some sections of the community. Liverpool Road was the first station built, but by 1844 the Manchester, Bury and Bolton Railway had built over the River Irwell and linked Salford with Manchester, eventually opening a station called Victoria by 1865. As was usual during the railway mania years, many other lines opened around this period, including the Manchester and Leeds Railway which in later years was to become part of the Lancashire and Yorkshire Railway. Also the Manchester and Cheshire Junction Railway was formed to construct a railway from Manchester to Crewe via Stockport; eventually this became the Manchester to Birmingham Railway, the line to Stockport opening in 1840. The Manchester terminus was situated in Travis Street. The terminus at London Road (Piccadilly as we know it today) was opened in 1842, and was jointly shared with the Sheffield, Ashton-Under-Lyne and Manchester Railway.

The other large station in Manchester was Central. The Cheshire Lines Committee had been pressing for its own independent terminus when it finally received permission in an Act of 1872 enabling it to build Central Station which was opened to the public in 1877. This was a temporary structure. The station opened properly in 1880 with a roof span of 210 feet, very similar in style to St.Pancras. From 6th March, 1967, local services on the former Midland main line through the Peak District were withdrawn with only CLC services to Liverpool and Chester in operation. The station eventually closed on 5th May, 1969, along with Exchange when all services were diverted to Victoria. Exchange was demolished and a car park built whilst Central, after lying derelict for twelve years, was converted into the G Mex Exhibition centre.

Recently a great deal has happened in the Manchester area, with the opening of the Hazel Grove chord and the Windsor Link in Salford. The Hazel Grove chord has linked the

8

Above: **The 18.55 Manchester Victoria to Liverpool Lime Street formed of Pacer Unit No.142051 is framed in the buffer stops at Ordsall Lane, Salford, as it crosses over the trackwork of the newly installed Windsor Link, which provides for the first time a direct train service between Blackpool North and East Anglia.**

Below: **The Salford skyscraper block makes Class 31/4 No. 31467 look diminutive as it passes over the new Windsor Link towards Ordsall Lane, Salford, with an empty TPO set on the afternoon of the 12th October, 1988. At the western end of the link a new station, Salford Crescent, has been built to cater for the student population of Salford University and the College of Technology.**

former LNWR line with the Midland line and was ready for the beginning of the May'86 timetable. The chord enabled Sheffield to Manchester trains to run into Piccadilly via Stockport instead of Marple and Manchester Victoria. The trains continue on to Liverpool to provide a better east-west service. The Windsor Link was opened at the beginning of the May'88 timetable and has linked the Lancashire and Yorkshire line from Bolton at Windsor Bridge Junction with the ex-LNWR line from Liverpool at Ordsall Lane, and has included the building of a new station at Salford Crescent to service Manchester University. With the commencement of the May 1989 timetable, InterCity trains are scheduled to run from Preston, Blackpool and Scotland into Piccadilly Station instead of Victoria. Another scheme presently underway in Manchester is the Light Rapid Transport System: the first stage will link Bury with Altrincham in the early 1990's. Electric trains, rather like the Docklands Railway in London, will be capable of travelling at 50 mph through city streets.

Manchester had pioneered an electrification scheme as long ago as 1913 under the Lancashire and Yorkshire Railway, when the Holcombe Brook branch was electrified at 3,500 volts supplied by overhead cables. The L & Y decided this system was too costly and implemented a third rail line between Victoria and Bury via Whitefield. This was a 1,200 volt DC system and is still in operation, having been inaugurated in April, 1916.

Passenger workings have been revitalised with the opening of the Windsor Link and the 'Express' service which was commissioned at the start of the May'88 timetable, again bringing Class 156 Sprinters on the East Anglia-North West workings. The Northenden Junction to Stockport route re-opened for passenger traffic at the start of the May'89 timetable bringing the Chester-Northwich-Manchester services over this route, a necessary diversion because it is hoped to make the Altrincham to Manchester line part of the Light Rapid Transport System. Because of this new routing the Greater Manchester P.T.E. are looking to build new stations in the Timperley-Wythenshawe areas.

Piccadilly is the principal station for the London workings which are in the hands of AC electric traction and run via Stoke-on-Trent. "The Manchester Pullman" is a popular service for the local business community. Class 47s have recently ousted the 'Peak' Class 45s from the Newcastle-Liverpool Trans-Pennine service which runs via Victoria but will soon be routed into Piccadilly. These services will be in the hands of Class 158 Express Units by the early 1990's.

In late 1988 a £9 million pound track and resignalling modernisation scheme took place at Piccadilly which renewed the 30-year-old equipment used by the London Road power box. At the same time remodelling of some track work took place to exploit the full potential of the new Windsor Link. This has also meant improving the route from Stalybridge and Guide Bridge, and extending platforms at Piccadilly and Oxford Road ready for the transfer of North Trans-Pennine trains as already mentioned. Four million pounds has also been invested in improving both Deansgate and Oxford Road stations and included platform lengthening for through InterCity trains and the installing of escalators at both stations.

On the freight side Trafford Park has a Freightliner Terminal with five scheduled departures each week day and two on a Saturday to destinations including, Holyhead Tilbury, and Crewe. There is also a Speedlink service connecting with Warrington Arpley Yard. Other workings of note include the Greater Manchester Refuse trains which run from Dean Lane to an infill site at Appley Bridge, near Wigan on the Southport line, the only freight traffic to use this ex-Lancashire and Yorkshire line; tar from the Tar Distillers Terminal at Weaste and Northenden which services the Blue Circle Cement works, and a chemical depot near Partington.

Opposite: **A busy scene on the 30th September, 1988, at the Oxford Road side of Manchester Piccadilly station as a major re-signalling and track realignment scheme gets under way. Class 86 No.86204 City of Carlisle is arriving with the 09.30 ex-London Euston. During this three week engineering period many timetable alterations were made with trains terminating at Stockport or being diverted in to Manchester Victoria. Oxford Road station was closed for the duration of the work which cost £9 million, but replaced signalling which was 30 years old and removed the bottleneck of lines which ran into Oxford Road.**

Below: **A panoramic view of the Manchester skyline from Ordsall Lane, Salford, as Class 31/1 No.31288 takes the Liverpool line with a long engineer's train, having just travelled through Victoria Station. The two lines in the left foreground form part of the new Windsor Link commissioned in May 1988 to facilitate the eventual transfer of Scottish through services to Manchester Piccadilly instead of Victoria, and also for the use of the new 'Express' services between Blackpool North and East Anglia. The G Mex Exhibition Centre can be seen to the right. To the left is the clock tower of Manchester Town Hall and the Granada TV Studios.**

Above: **Class 504 Bury 3rd rail electric unit No.M77167 approaches Crumpsall signal cabin with the 12.15 ex-Bury on the 28th October, 1988.** The line to Bury from Manchester Victoria serves the heart of commuter land, and services run every 15 minutes during the peak period and every 30 minutes off peak. There is, however, no Sunday service. This line was electrified in April 1916 by the Lancashire and Yorkshire Railway, and was a pioneering scheme for its time.

Below: **The setting winter's sun catches the side of a Class 304 electric unit forming the 14.30 Manchester Piccadilly to Hadfield as it approaches Dinting on the afternoon of the 28th October, 1988.** This used to be the through Woodhead route which was closed between Hadfield and Penistone in 1981, the overhead system being converted from 1500dc to 25kv in 1984. The abandoned area in the foreground was originally Mottram yard, which closed in the middle 70's and has now reverted to 'mother nature'.

Warrington, Wigan and Preston

Warrington, Wigan and Preston, are Lancashire towns associated during the booming Industrial Revolution with the wire, coal and cotton manufacturing trades. Today, however, Warrington has only two wire manufacturers, although the town's Rugby League team is still nicknamed "The Wires". Wigan has no coal mines, although the surrounding area has three large pits linked underground; Preston still has many mills, though they no longer produce cotton. However, a common denominator linking the three towns today as it did 150 years ago, is the railway.

The first railway came to Warrington on the 25th July, 1831, and was known as the Warrington and Newton Railway which, as its name suggests, linked the towns. It ran for 4½ miles and employed three steam locomotives built by Stephenson and named "Warrington", "Newton" and "Vulcan". From the latter is the name of the modern Vulcan Foundry at Newton-le-Willows, now operated by GEC Traction Ltd. The Warrington and Newton Railway was eventually taken over by the Grand Junction Railway which built the line from Warrington to Birmingham, later to become part of the LNWR. Other lines constructed during this period included the Warrington and Altrincham Junction Railway of 1851 which was to become the Warrington and Stockport Railway of 1853. These lines again were incorporated into the LNWR. Bank Quay station was opened in 1868 but Arpley on the low-level line was closed, much to the disgust of the local townspeople who found the low-level station more convenient than Bank Quay. In fact Arpley station reopened three years later and eventually closed in 1958. The station area is now occupied by the BR Area Manager's Office. The other Warrington station, known as Central, was part of the Cheshire Lines Committee. It opened for passengers in 1873, and is still in use today on the Liverpool to Manchester route.

Ten miles north of Warrington on the WCML lies the old mining town of Wigan, whose history can be traced back to the 12th Century. Steam engines had been used in the local colliery yards as early as 1812 and coal had greatly advanced the prosperity of Wigan although today the town has no pits to call its own. Coal had been discovered in the 14th Century but was not mined commercially until the 18th century when it was transported to Liverpool for shipment abroad by means of the Leeds and Liverpool Canal completed by 1780. By this time, many of the local pits, including the Stone House Colliery near Pemberton, had built their own rail lines to link with the canal. The colliery erected a pierhead at the canal in Wigan from which the famous Wigan Pier name originated, the complex today being a popular tourist attraction.

In 1832, the Wigan Branch Railway was the

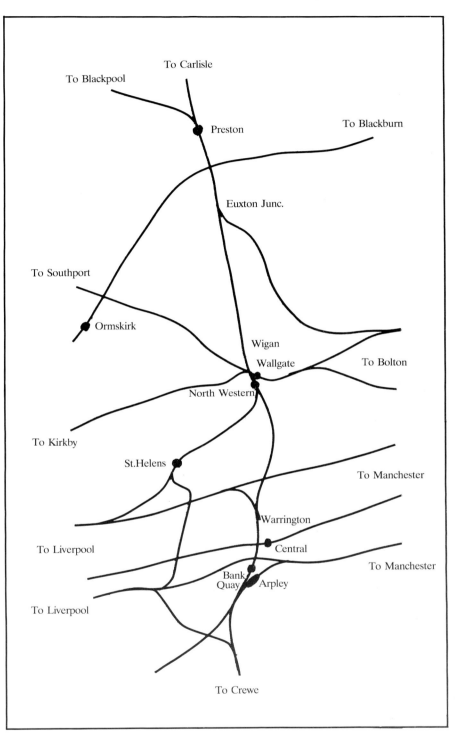

first company to lay tracks in Wigan when it opened its line from Parkside Junction (near Newton-le-Willows) to Chapel Lane in the town. Two years later the company amalgamated with the Preston and Wigan Company to form the North Union Railway which in 1838 reached Preston. Wigan North Western station opened in 1888, and is still a principal station on the WCML between Euston and Glasgow. Wigan also boasted two other stations, one on the Lancashire and Yorkshire line in Wallgate, and the Cheshire Lines Committee (later Great Central) station known as Central. The first Wallgate station was opened in May 1860 but was criticised by the local corporation, and was eventually closed in 1896 when the present Wallgate station was opened. The CLC station was opened at a temporary terminus in Darlington Street in 1884, and in 1892 an extension of a ¼ mile was opened to Wigan Central. Passenger services were withdrawn in 1964 and the site has become a municipal car park. There are no telltale signs of the CLC involvement with Wigan except for bridge abutments by the River Douglas.

The modern day rail traveller can leave Wigan on the fastest train of the day and arrive at Preston 15 minutes later. Preston's first rail lines arrived in 1838 from Parkside Junction by courtesy of the North Union Railway, an amalgamation of the Wigan Branch and the Preston and Wigan Railway. The public opening on 31st October, 1838, gave Preston a link with London. With the coming of the NUR many other companies were formed to link up with the main line at Preston, including the Preston and Wyre, the Preston and Bolton, the Preston and Longridge and the Preston and Lancaster Junction Railway which was to push the WCML further north. There was also the Liverpool, Ormskirk and Preston Railway along with the East Lancashire Railway which had absorbed the Blackburn and Preston Railway. The ELR had its own platforms at Preston, renting space from the NUR. Besides the NUR station in Preston, the West Lancashire Railway had constructed its own terminus at the bottom of Fishergate Hill which was opened in 1882 and closed 82 years later in 1964 as another casualty of the Beeching cuts. Nothing today remains of the terminus as new sheltered accommodation for old people has been built on the site.

Fishergate station built by the NUR and still in use today on the WCML was reconstructed in 1880 at the cost of £250,000, its most striking feature being the large island platforms which today are numbered 3 and 4, platform 3 taking the northbound trains and platform 4 the southbound. In 1972 the East Lancashire platforms were removed, and this area has become yet another car park, serving a large retail store. Electrification came to Preston on 23rd July, 1973, when through-working was authorised between Euston and Glasgow.

In 1989 there is plenty for the modern traction enthusiast to see in the area encompassing the WCML between Warrington and Preston. Warrington itself is a hive of activity with most work centering around Arpley and Walton Old Junction Speedlink Yards. The yards operate three eight-hour shifts 24-hours a day and train loads arrive from all over the country from Willesden, Doncaster, Healey Mills, Peak Forest, and Mossend amongst others. Typically, on the 30th June, 1988, there were 44 arrivals and 47 departures from the yards including Speedlink feeder services and trip work. Since the closure of Crewe Basford Hall Yard in the early 1970's, Warrington has taken over the marshalling of all freight traffic in the North West and North Wales areas. The 20 roads at Arpley deal mainly with the 'up' traffic whilst the smaller Walton Old Junction yard deals with the 'down' traffic on 13 roads. The yards receive plenty of trip work including coal from the local collieries, seven each way from Bickershaw near Wigan, and two each way from Parkside Colliery, Newton-le-Willows to Fidlers Ferry Power Station on the outskirts of Warrington. Other trip work dealt with includes chemicals from ICI at Folly Lane, Runcorn, fertilisers from UKF at Ince and Elton, petroleum products from both Shell and Associated Octel plants in Ellesmere Port, and additional chemical traffic from ICI at Burn Naze, near Thornton Cleveleys on the Fylde coast.

On the passenger side Warrington Bank Quay is a principal station on the WCML and despatches numerous departures to both Euston and Glasgow as well as serving the cross-country route between Leeds, Manchester and North Wales. Main line services are hauled by electric traction, usually Classes 86, 87 and 90, whilst the cross-country route is served by Class 150 sprinters. After the closure of Dallam Steam Shed in 1967 the depot was refurbished and taken over by an engineering firm. the depot still stands today by the WCML just north of Warrington although it is not easily recognisable as a steam MPD. Diesel locomotives now stable at Arpley by the side of the Speedlink yard and adjacent to the old Cheshire Lines Committee low-level route to Manchester, whilst electric traction stable in both the north and south bays at Bank Quay station.

Wigan still has two stations, North Western on the WCML and Wallgate on the Manchester-Kirkby-Southport routes. Both stations are well patronised and in return give a good service to the travelling public. Wigan can still boast a Motive Power Depot at Springs Branch. Springs Branch only has an allocation of Class 08 shunters but many visiting locomotives use the depot for fuelling after arriving at Warrington Arpley on Speedlink duties. The depot is also authorised to carry out both A and B exams which it regularly does on the Toton Class 20s out-

Back to the turn of the century when all engine movements had to be preceded by a man with a red flag! But this picture happens to have been taken in 1988. Class 56 No.56093 is a rare visitor to the Preston Docks Branch, where it is crossing over Strand Road for its journey back up the 1 in 29 gradient to the WCML at Preston station with the 7E60 to Lindsay Oil Refinery. The branch originated in 1846, and was used by the North Union Railway to convey coal from the pits of Wigan to the quays by the River Ribble. The actual docks complex only opened in 1892, and closed in 1981. Much of the area is now devoted to a marina and shopping complex. However, the oil terminal was retained on a simplified track layout and is used for storage as distribution is made by road. In the background can be seen part of the Strand Road Works of English Electric (now GEC Traction) where the prototype Deltic was built.

Above: **Class 20 Nos.20078 and 20080 double-head the 7F62 Point of Ayr to Fidlers Ferry coal train on the 15th April, 1988 past the modern signal box at Mickle Trafford. It is here that the Warrington and Northwich routes meet on their journey west to Chester. Point of Ayr is the only surviving colliery in North Wales, and despatches just one train load of coal per day to Fidlers Ferry.**

Below: **20th May, 1988. A mixture of 1st generation DMU designs form the 18.48 Manchester Oxford Road to Warrington Central against a darkening sky at Irlam on the ex-Cheshire Lines Committee route between Manchester and Liverpool.**

Above: A busy scene at Springs Branch Junction just south of Wigan as Class 20 Nos.20121 and 20004 draw past the 7T75 which is waiting to depart up the Bickershaw branch hauled by a further two Class 20 Nos.20084 and 20078. Bickershaw Colliery is one of only two rail-connected pits in the much-reduced Lancashire coalfield, and is situated on the truncated ex-LNW route between Wigan and Manchester via Tyldesley. The pit despatches 7 trains a day to Fidlers Ferry Power Station, near Warrington, and 3 on Saturday mornings, giving an annual output of 2½ million tonnes.

Centre: The 19.07 Manchester Victoria to Southport rumbles across the Leeds-Liverpool Canal heading for Wigan Wallgate in the hands of a Class 108 DMU. The church spire is that of St.Catharine's and is the tallest in the Wigan diocese.

Below: The low evening sun highlights Class 87 No.87002 Royal Sovereign running through Wigan with the 16.20 Glasgow Central to Birmingham on 24th June, 1988. The church in the background is All Saints' Parish Church, the tower of which dates back to the 13th Century.

An impressive line-up of electric power at Preston on Christmas Day, 1988. Leading the six engines is Class 81 No.81017. More than half of this vintage class of electrics have been withdrawn from service. Next is Class 86/2 No.86248 Sir Clwyd/County of Clwyd in revised InterCity livery, then Class 85 No.85037 in Standard Rail Blue, Class 90 No.90003 in the new Swallow InterCity livery, Class 86/4 No.86439 in revised InterCity livery, and finally, Class 87 No.87035 Robert Burns in Standard Rail Blue.

stabled at the depot for the local Bickershaw to Fidlers Ferry coal runs. In the past Wigan had two other sheds, one in Prescot Street belonging to the Lancashire and Yorkshire Railway (closed 1964), the other in Higher Ince run by the Great Central Company (closed 1952). A supermarket now stands on the site of the Great Central shed, whilst the building in Prescot Street is still standing but in a derelict condition, its last known use being a stores depot for the electrification train.

Next stop north on the WCML is Preston, a town which has recently celebrated 150 years of railway history. The station is of considerable size with six platforms including bays at the south end. A variety of lines still converges on Preston including the Ormskirk to Preston line which is now a glorified branch having once been the 'through express' route to Liverpool. It is now truncated at Ormskirk where passengers have to change onto the MerseyRail electrics to travel on to Liverpool. The Blackpool lines run in by the WCML at the north end of the station by St.Walburge's Church which has the second highest spire in the country after Salisbury Cathedral, and the Blackburn and East Lancashire lines run in from the east through Lostock Hall where the station was reopened in 1985.

Lostock Hall MPD was one of the last three steam depots to remain operative in 1968, and in fact supplied the motive power for BR's last day of steam on the 3rd of August. The depot is still standing but in a dilapidated condition. Preston also had its own steam shed but its early demise was brought about in 1961 when the depot was engulfed by fire which destroyed the roof and damaged some engines, including 7Fs 49104 and 49382 and Standard Class 2, 78037. A newspaper report of the time states "the heat was so intense inside the depot that the metal rails just buckled". The site has now been cleared and is occupied at the north end by the power signal box commissioned in 1973 at the start of the electric service between Euston and Glasgow.

Diesel engines stable at Ladywell Sidings just north of the station (partially visible from the WCML), electric traction uses sidings at the south end (visible from passing trains) whilst DMU's stable by the power box (also visible from the main line).

A large variety of motive power can be seen at Preston besides the Inter City electrics with Classes, 20, 31, 37, and 47s to the fore. Even a Class 26 can be seen interloping from the Scottish region on the Wednesday-only van train from Carlisle. Scottish based Class 37s are regularly seen double-heading the Clitheroe to Gunnie, Glasgow cement train through the station.

During the summer of 1988, haulage bashers had a field day because of the shortage of Sprinters and Pacers mainly on the Blackpool North to Manchester Victoria, and Preston to Liverpool routes. Class 31s and Class 47s, including the Railfreight variety with no heating facilities have filled in on these turns. British Rail stated at the time that the problem would be sorted out by the start of the winter timetable but still no heat locomotives were operating during the winter months much to the annoyance of the travelling public who have been conveyed in 'ice boxes'.

With the Class 90s now established on the WCML route, the area between Warrington and Preston holds a great deal of excitement for the modern traction enthusiast.

Left: The ornate platform awnings frame a Class 108 DMU at Warrington Central Station after its arrival from Liverpool Lime Street with the 08.14 local service. Central Station lies on the old Cheshire Lines Committee route between Manchester and Liverpool and is a very busy commuter station with as many as 30 workings each way, Monday to Friday. A new frontage was built onto the station three years ago rendering the original Cheshire Lines booking office redundant, but still intact.

Above:. With snowploughs attached and standing in pouring rain, Class 26 No.26025 waits in Preston station with the 3P13 Wednesdays only parcels working from Carlisle. This is now a common Class 26 working and must be the furthest south that this class of Scottish Region locomotives work. On this particular occasion, within 10 minutes of its arrival, the Class 26 returned north light engine, almost as if it were homesick!

Below: Overshadowed by the ornate chimneys and structure of the County Hall, Preston, Class 85 No.85024 shunts TPO stock whilst station pilot Class 08 No.08744 is stabled in the parcels bay platform between duties. The 08 which is allocated to Springs Branch TMD, Wigan has recently been painted by depot staff and is in a clean external condition, complete with white painted handrails and red buffer beam.

Above: The driver of the first Class 90 No.90001, checks for the guards green flag as he prepares to leave Platform 2 at Preston Station on a north bound test train of Mark 2 coaches for Glasgow Central. InterCity trains normally use Platforms 3 and 4 at Preston, Platform 2 being reserved for Blackpool to Manchester, and Preston to Colne trains.

Right: Viewed from the steeple of St.Walburge's church, the up and down "Royal Scots" pass just north of Preston Station on the 28th December, 1988. The spire at 303 feet, is second tallest in England to Salisbury Cathedral. St.Walburge's also has stone sleepers from the Lancaster and Preston Junction Railway incorporated in the lower portion if its steeple. The 'up' train is the 10.25 Glasgow Central to Euston, whilst the 'down' working is the 10.30 Euston to Glasgow Central. Both trains are on the WCML, the line to the right being the non-electrified route to Blackpool North and South via Kirkham.

The line curving away to the left by the 'up' electric locomotive is the truncated Longridge Branch built to carry stone from Longridge Fell to Preston Docks. The line closed to passengers as early as 1930, although freight continued to use the branch through to Longridge until 1967. Today the line serves a coal yard at Deepdale which sees the occasional trip working to Warrington Arpley Speedlink Yard. The multiple-units are stabled on the site of the former steam depot which had to close prematurely in 1961 after fire engulfed the building damaging a number of steam engines as well as destroying the roof. The shed was later used to store condemned steam engines. A Class 90 can just be seen at the head of a short empty stock train, and just to the right of the units is the Preston Power Box which opened in February 1973 in readiness for the through electrification between Preston and Glasgow Central which commenced in May 1974. Preston station which celebrated its 150th anniversary in 1988 is just beyond the bridge in the centre of the picture.

The Cumbrian Coast

Cumbria, with its considerable natural resources of iron ore, heralded the birth of the railways in this part of the country. By the mid 1800's, 40,000 tons of iron ore were being shipped monthly through the port of Barrow, and so it was that James Walker, the President of the Institute of Civil Engineers, was asked to construct a railway link from the iron mines at Dalton to the harbour in Barrow. On the basis of Walker's reports, all the local iron producing mines requested to be linked to Barrow as well. This brought about the formation of the Furness Railway which was granted an Act of Parliament incorporating the line on 23rd May, 1844. The main trunk route of the line was constructed south west from Lindal to Dalton-in-Furness, and on to Barrow. The line ran close to the ruins of Furness Abbey, a state of affairs which annoyed the eminent poet Wordsworth, who was said to be, "horrified at the desecration being wreaked by the Furness Railway Company".

The first locomotives for the line were supplied by a company in Liverpool and had to be shipped, lashed to the decks of tugboats, from Fleetwood across Morecambe Bay, there being no rail connection to the WCML of the Lancaster and Carlisle Railway at Carnforth. Passenger services commenced running between Barrow and Dalton on the 12th August, 1846, but were of a very simple nature. They conveyed, however, over 1,500 passengers on various trains through the day. An extension to Broughton authorised on the 27th July, 1846, and opening in February, 1848, brought in revenue from the Coniston Copper mines situated within the Lake District, which at that time had not realised its tourist potential. By 1849 iron ore was being carried at the rate of 600 tons a day to the iron works of South Wales, via shipment from Barrow, and by 1850 this figure had trebled.

By the early 1840's the Furness Railway system was still isolated from other major routes, but in 1844 the Maryport and Carlisle Railway had built an extension southwards via Whitehaven Junction which eventually meant the forming of a new company to be known as the Whitehaven and Furness Junction Railway which constructed a line southwards through St.Bees and Seascale, running close by the sea. Although an important communication link had been formed by the W & F Junction Railway, the final missing link of the chain to the south was to be forged by the formation of the Ulverston and Lancaster Railway by an Act of Parliament in 1851. The line officially opened on 7th June, 1854, passing south from Ulverston through Grange-over-Sands, Arnside and on to Carnforth. At the northern end of the line timber viaducts had to be constructed over the rivers Calder, Irt, Mite, Esk and Duddon. The names of Irt and Mite are now carried by engines on the narrow gauge Ravenglass and Eskdale Railway which was originally built to transport iron ore to the coast, but is run as a privately preserved line. Stations opened along this new section of line included St.Bees, Nethertown, Sellafield, Seascale, Drigg, Ravenglass and Eskmeals.

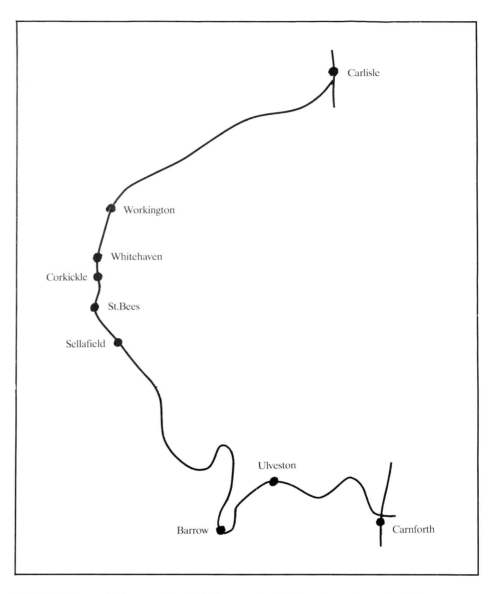

By the end of the 18th Century, Barrow had become a boom town because of its impressive docks complex which was shipping iron ore all over the world, but the Furness Railway in its wisdom did not rest on its laurels. Instead it realised that a tourist potential existed with their railway running so close to the Lake District and also along the shoreline of Morecambe Bay. By the late 1860's the company had encouraged a great deal of tourist traffic and therefore, by Edwardian times, when this was at its busiest, the company did not feel the effects of the rapidly diminishing iron ore trade. The Furness Railway managed to remain independent until the 1923 amalgamations when it became part of the LMS.

It was during Edwardian times that cockles fished from the River Kent estuary were despatched by rail from Kents Bank station to destinations all over the country. Horse drawn carts, later tractor-drawn, would go out into Morecambe Bay at low tide to collect the cockles which were bagged and put on to the nightly 'fish' train. Today, unfortunately, this traffic goes by road!

The Whitehaven and Furness Railways' northern section of line had also stimulated a resort development at St.Bees, and a special halt had been constructed to serve the local golf course. The Company also planned for a large resort at Seascale with a grand hotel, promenade and marine walks, but with the town being miles from the largest conurbations these plans were severely curtailed, as even the railway could not bring in the large numbers of people needed to make the development pay. If the proposed building had gone ahead it would have been interesting to see if the large nuclear power station at Sellafield, built in 1956 by the United Kingdom Energy Authority (now British Nuclear Fuels Ltd.), would have been given the go-ahead. The complex when first built was known as Calder Hall, and it brought new lifeblood to the area. Sellafield station was rebuilt and a small branch constructed to serve the plant. Some believe the building of the power station saved the Barrow to Whitehaven line from closure. Today nuclear flask traffic still serves the site some 30 years after its construction and, of course, passenger traffic still uses the line. Until 1986 the line was also used by the Cumbrian Mountain Pullman steam-hauled specials, and passengers used to disembark at Ravenglass for the local narrow gauge line.

The whole Cumbrian coast route was served by just three Motive Power depots situated at Barrow (ex-Furness Railway and situated in the dock complex near the Furness Railway Works), Moor Row, Whitehaven (a joint LNWR-Furness Railway depot), and Workington which was always a LNWR shed. Moor Row closed in 1954, Barrow in 1966 and Workington at the beginning of 1968. In 1950, Barrow had an allocation of 50 engines including 2Fs, 2Ps, 4Fs and Black Fives; Moor Row only had twelve locomotives on its books of the 3F and 4F freight types. Workington had 27 locomotives, again all being of the freight variety. Barrow shed also had the Class 28 Co-Bo Metrovick diesels on its books which finished their short 10-year life-span working from here on local freight and passenger turns, including the Lakeside Branch connecting with the Lake Windermere sailings. At present, locomotives stable at the north end of Barrow Station, the only stabling point on the entire Cumbrian Coast route.

On the freight scene the situation is encouraging, for regular traffic operates over the entire 114 mile route. Coal is taken from Lakeland Colliery (Maryport) to Fidlers Ferry Power station near Warrington once a day, whilst there are two scheduled trip workings to Workington Docks for export. This colliery is the only one operating in the whole of Cumbria. Chemical traffic originates from the ICI works at Folly Lane, Runcorn, destined for the chemical complex at Corkickle just outside Whitehaven. There is also a Speedlink service between Workington and Willesden, running as the 6A40 16.58 from Workington, and the 6P85 22.15 from Willesden. This is a Class 47 diagram to Preston, with electric traction taking over there for the run down the WCML. The train stops at Warrington Arpley Speedlink yard en route to attach other traffic. From the Carnforth end of the line various trips run "as and when required", and include household coal to Barrow, cement to Sellafield and oil to Ulverston. The British Nuclear Fuel Power Station at Sellafield deals with low grade nuclear waste traffic including the 7P40 from Valley (Anglesey) to Sellafield which connects into a working at Llandudno Junction from the Trawsfynydd Nuclear Power Station. Flasks are also brought to Sellafield from Bridgewater, Winfrith, Dungeness and via Barrow docks.

Passenger traffic is in the hands of aged DMUs, usually Derby Works Class 108s. Workings in the south originate from Preston and run to Barrow. Until a few years ago there was a through working from London (Euston) to Barrow but this has now been rescheduled to start from Birmingham New Street, running on Fridays only. From the northern end of the line at Carlisle there is a service via Whitehaven and Workington to Barrow. The line has had no real investment for several years, but the passenger trains are still well patronised with 6 workings each way (Monday to Saturday) between Carlisle and Barrow. The Preston to Barrow service fares much better with over 20 services each way between the two towns (Monday to Saturday). On Sundays the service begins at Lancaster with six workings each way.

If the nuclear flask traffic were to be run down or the power station at Sellafield suddenly to close, the Cumbrian Coast Route would find itself staring closure in the face. But whilst the important freight traffic is still operating at its present level the future of the line looks secure.

Running across the flats of the Duddon Estuary between Askam-in-Furness and Kirby-in-Furness is the 10.30 Barrow-in-Furness to Carlisle two-car DMU working on the 10th December, 1988. On the far bank of the meandering River Duddon is the town of Millom whilst to the right of the picture Black Combe Fell is enveloped in low cloud on this bright but cold winter's day.

Right: The semaphore signals at Corkickle make a fine spectacle as the early morning mist rises to reveal the 10.30 Barrow-in-Furness to Carlisle train passing with an incorrect destination blind showing Millom which had been passed nine stations previously! Corkickle is a busy freight point just south of Whitehaven from where trains are despatched by Speedlink services. In the main, they comprise of phosphoric acid and tripolyphosphate loaded wagons bound for Ince UKF, Warrington and Grays in Essex. Note the man on the nearest signal gantry re-filling the oil lamps.

Below: Working the 13.50 Barrow-in-Furness to Carlisle, a 1st generation DMU trundles passed the small signal box at Drigg on the Cumbrian Coast Line on a bitterly cold day in January 1989. The Lake District Fells in the background are still managing to be covered in low cloud even though the sun is bright, but, alas, not too warm! The box at Drigg controls the level crossing gate (the signalman opens and closes the gate by hand!) and cross over points, as well as a siding which serves a storage depot for British Nuclear Fuels Ltd., and is used once a week by a trip from Sellafield.

Above: A Class 108 DMU forming the 11.55 Carlisle to Barrow service passes the UK Atomic Energy Authority's works at Sellafield on the Cumbrian Coast line. The plant was commissioned in 1956 and was firstly known as Calder Hall. Sidings were laid into the complex to cater for the Nuclear Waste traffic which still runs today from various locations throughout the British Isles. The land to the right is Seascale Golf Course and is very popular with the workforce at Sellafield, being literally on the plant's doorstep.

Below: Class 31/4 No.31425 pictured at St.Bees with the 17.53 Workington to Huddersfield TPO train. This is the smallest TPO run by the Post Office, and consists of just one sorting van and two stowage vehicles. Until recently, the working used a variety of Class 47 power. Now Class 31s have taken over with the same locomotive used all week. The train stops at Barrow, Lancaster, Preston and Manchester during its journey to Yorkshire.

Carlisle, The Border City

At the beginning of the 18th Century Carlisle had become a booming textile town with a population of around 8,000, its links with the rest of the country maintained by the various mail and stage coaches.

The first railway line to reach the town was not the north-to-south route as could be expected but an east-to-west one, namely the Newcastle and Carlisle Railway which was incorporated by an Act of Parliament in 1829, and opened to the public seven years later on 19th July, 1836. The line, on opening, had its terminus at London Road in Carlisle (later named Citadel and known today simply as Carlisle) and ran to Greenhead in Northumberland. Some eastern sections of the line had already been completed and so it was that, on the 18th June, 1838, the route was opened throughout to Gateshead to complete the east-west link. Coal as well as passengers had become an important revenue-earning commodity from the early days of the line, being despatched from Blenkinsop Colliery near Greenhead for export via Port Carlisle

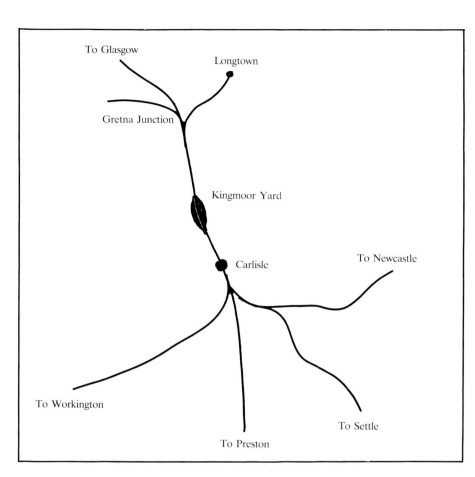

The 09.45 Euston to Stranraer Harbour train pulls into a busy Carlisle station at precisely 14.17, 14 minutes down on its booked arrival time. The locomotive is Class 86/2 No.86230 The Duke of Wellington, one of the last of the class to remain in overall blue livery. The electric engine will be detached at Carlisle in favour of a Class 47 for the remainder of its journey to Stranraer.

A surprise visitor to Carlisle on the 22nd October, 1988 was the celebrity chocolate and cream liveried Class 117 Pressed Steel Surburban unit based at Tyseley. The Unit formed of cars, 51368, 59520 and 51410 had worket into Carlisle from Walsall in the West Midlands with the curiously named "Weymouth Nose Poker"!

(previously known as Fishers Cross) to Ireland and Scotland. At that time England had no rail link to Scotland and the easiest way to transport coal was by sea.

Until 1846 the most direct route to London, if it could be so called, was via Newcastle and the East Coast Main Line, but on 17th December, 1846, the West Coast route arrived in the town bringing the people of Carlisle a more direct and quicker route to London.

By the mid 1800's, seven companies were operating from Carlisle Citadel station, including the Maryport and Carlisle, the Lancaster and Carlisle (later the LNWR), the North Eastern, the Midland, the Caledonian, the North British, and the Glasgow and South Western. This of course caused endless problems for the operating department not only because of the complex nature of train movements, but also because the Companies themselves were forever quarrelling about which should have preferential treatment.

The station was made even busier by the many through services which stopped there for extended refreshment breaks. Trains did not operate Refreshment Cars, and the platforms were overcrowded with weary travellers taking sustenance!

Citadel was designed by the Lancaster and Carlisle Railway's architect, Sir William Tite, and was built in a mock Tudor style with a large clock tower. The station entrance had a five bay arcade with three mullion windows displaying the heraldic coats-of-arms of the Lancaster and Carlisle Railway, and the Caledonian Railway. It has been alleged that the other two windows were left blank because the Newcastle and Carlisle, and the Maryport and Carlisle Railways, had never really seen eye to eye with the other companies.

By 1847 the station was in joint ownership of the Lancaster and Carlisle, and the Caledonian Railways, and £60,000 had been spent on the station by the English Company, a fact that had not gone unnoticed by the company's directors. It was not until 1854 that the Scottish Company began to help financially with station improvements when it contributed half of a £178,324 bill to help with the upkeep of the station. The reason for the Scottish Company's reluctance to pay was made known in 1850 when The Times newspaper pointed out "the reckless expansion programme the Company had pursued to fortify its position in gaining a route to the south via the Newcastle and Carlisle Railway, leaving the Company short of capital".

By the early 1860's it became clear that the vice-like grip on Carlisle by the Lancaster and Carlisle, (later LNWR) and the Caledonian Railway Companies would have to be loosened if the other railway companies were to get a fair deal. The North British had spent £5 million (a great deal of money in 1860) on its Waverley route to find its West Coast partners (namely the Lancaster and Carlisle, and the Caledonian) blockading the route, making it little more than an expensive branch line to Scotland. Tactics included holding the North British services at Carlisle until Caledonian passenger trains had departed, and failing to forward northbound goods.

Eventually the Carlisle Goods Traffic Committee was formed to look after the interests of the other companies using Carlisle, which made the Caledonian's delaying tactics a thing of the past.

By 1880 Carlisle was a major centre of the railway system with flows of traffic which were to increase greatly in the coming years. But the problem which occurred here, as well as at other rail centres, was that the large companies tended to sit back and do nothing to meet changing circumstances, something the town would suffer for until the modern rail scene arrived.

The station had become a bottleneck with only three through roads, (the same as in 1989), although today's traffic is far less, and more manageable. But in the late 1800's a great deal of delay was encountered within the station area with many trains being held outside the station awaiting suitable platform space. Passenger traffic was not helped by the heavy volume of freight which had to pass through Carlisle. This had reached a peak in November 1917, when 200,000 wagons a week were passing through. To monitor the situation a Joint Control was set up to check goods traffic and allow passenger services priority routing. It was not until 1943 that a loop line around the station was opened from Carlisle No.3 signalbox to Kingmoor Yard. This line in fact closed in 1986 owing to a fall in freight traffic within the Carlisle area, and trains now pass through the centre roads at Carlisle.

By the late 1950's only three engine sheds had survived in the area, these being Kingmoor, Upperby and Canal. By this time freight wagons passing through Carlisle had dropped to 30,000 a week. Canal MPD had closed by 1963, with Upperby succumbing by 1966. Steam 'died' in Carlisle on 31st December, 1967, when Kingmoor MPD closed and all work transferred to the new diesel depot built opposite on the west side of the main line. The closure of Kingmoor also meant the end of steam working over Shap. The last steam working from Kingmoor was the 13.10 Carlisle to Skipton goods hauled by Britannia Pacific No.70045 *Lord Rowallan*. Upperby is still in use today as a carriage servicing depot and also sees the occasional steam engine which has worked in over the Settle and Carlisle route. The depot still retains an ash pit and watering facilities for such special workings. Canal shed has been demolished and Kingmoor steam depot has reverted to nature with young saplings growing where Black 5s, Coronations, and Britannia Pacifics once stood. In the last days of steam all the Britannias were shedded at Kingmoor, eking out their last hours on local trip and the occasional football special workings. The new Kingmoor Diesel Depot is now also closed, a sad sign of the times, and whilst the diesel servicing shed in Kingmoor yard still stands, it is devoid of any permanent way. Visiting locos now stable in the station area or at High Wapping sidings to the south of the station.

Kingmoor's small fleet of Class 08 shunters have been transferred to Carlisle Upperby. One shunter still works Kingmoor Yard, a far cry from the days when six shunters worked the transfer sidings. Another is station pilot, and also performs local trip work to Upperby for the cement works. A further one is outstabled at Workington to service the British Steel Corporations complex, only returning to Carlisle for maintenance on a monthly basis. A few years ago one of Kingmoor's Class 08s was outstabled at Dumfries, the only English depot with a shunter working in Scotland!

The huge Kingmoor Marshalling Yard was commissioned in 1959 at a cost of £4½ million and was part of the BR Modernisation Scheme. It was built to the north of Carlisle in an area 2½ miles long by ¼ mile wide. It was designed to handle 5,600 wagons a day in 123 sidings covering 56 miles of track, but with traffic having changed to Speedlink and block Company trains, the yard is but a shadow of its former self. A power box was also constructed at the same time and covered an area from Carlisle No.3 box to Gretna on the Scottish border. This was superseded in 1973 by a new power box to the south of Carlisle station, built in conjunction with the WCML electrification scheme, and covering 74 miles of track from Oxenholme in the south to Kirkpatrick in Scotland. The new box also covers the Maryport line, the Annan line and some five miles of the Midland and Newcastle approaches.

Still of interest to the modern traction enthusiast is the working of Scottish based locomotives into the city; these now of course are restricted to Class 26 and 47, the Class 26s being the only 'pure' Scottish motive power.

Passenger workings see a variety of power with the modern AC Electric engines on the Anglo-Scottish services and Class 47s on the Settle and Carlisle route. Class 47s also work the Stranraer boat trains to and from Carlisle. First generation DMUs, usually Class 108s, work the Whitehaven, Workington and Barrow services, whilst Class 156 Sprinters are appearing on through services from the Newcastle area to Glasgow and Ayr.

The freight scene has expanded again in recent years even though Kingmoor Yard has been scaled down to make the yard more profitable. The yard, which is part of the Speedlink network, services 16 trains a day, including some cross country services between Newcastle (Tyne Yard) and Stranraer. Trip working is very important in the area with services converging from various places including Dumfries (fuel oil and timber), Eastriggs, Longtown and Brunthill (Ministry of Defence). At Brunthill, the only remains of the North British "Waverley Route", closed in January 1969, is a spur into the military depot. At the northern end of the Waverley Route, Millerhill yard contains the only visible remains of this former prestigious Anglo-Scottish link. Other trip workings into Kingmoor originate from the cement works at Upperby, and mixed goods workings from Workington and Wigton.

153 years after the railway arrived in Carlisle the station is still an important 'bridging' point between England and Scotland, and modern railway observers can still enjoy a few hours train watching in the impressive train shed which is truly the gateway to Scotland in the "Border City".

The driver of Class 86/2 No.86239 L.S.Lowry pauses awhile in the middle road at Carlisle station, taking in the bright autumn sunlight as he awaits a clear signal to Upperby depot to the south of the station. His attention had been drawn by WC Class No.34092 City of Wells which was working a special over the Settle and Carlisle route to Preston. In the background a Class 108 DMU waits in the bay with the 14.50 departure to Barrow. The date of the photograph was 22nd October, 1988.

Above: An aptly named locomotive, Class 86 No.86204 City of Carlisle pictured appropriately enough in the City of Carlisle. The locomotive was working the 23.50 Glasgow Central to Euston "The Night Caledonian", and had stopped at Carlisle in the early hours of the 22nd September, 1988, for a crew change. The train name links back to the late 1800's when the Caledonian was one of the seven railway companies converging on Carlisle.

Below: Carlisle Station stands silent and deserted at 23.35 hours on the evening of 22nd September, 1988, except for a lone Class 08 shunter No.08912 on station pilot duties. A few years ago three Class 08s were employed at Citadel Station on such duties. Nowadays one shunter suffices.

The Settle and Carlisle

The Settle and Carlisle route epitomises man's efforts to conquer the greatest of physical challenges, especially as the line was built over one hundred years ago when the mainstay of labour was the navvy.

A proposed Act of Parliament signed on 16th July, 1866, authorised the construction of the 72 mile long route, but in 1867 the bill was rejected and a worried Midland Railway Board instructed contractors not to begin work on the line. The Bill had been rejected by Parliament because of the suspicions surrounding the merger of the Midland with the Glasgow and South-Western Railway, suspicions which proved unfounded. So it was that pressure was brought to bear by the Lancashire and Yorkshire and the North British Railways for construction of the line by the Midland Company, thus giving both companies through routes between England and Scotland. Building began in November 1869, with J.S. Crossley as engineer after the line had been surveyed by a pioneer called Sharland from Tasmania, who planned the route with 1 in 100 gradients. One of Sharland's bases during the survey was the Gearstones Inn, eleven miles from Settle, where he remained snowbound for three weeks, no doubt enjoying the enforced hospitality of the inn!

The Settle and Carlisle was the last great trunk route to be built by the traditional navvy method, and in 1871 at the height of construction, it employed over 7,000 men and 500 horses. Shanty towns appeared between Settle and Appleby, the largest being at Batty Green, near Ribblehead Viaduct, and included a community serviced by pubs, shops, a hospital, a Post Office and mission house, although the last apparently saw little use! By 1873 when the line was scheduled for completion, only 3¾ miles between Settle and Stainforth was serviceable. By the 2nd August, 1875, though, freight traffic was operating over the entire route, and the line was officially opened to passengers on 1st May, 1876, but without a ceremony. The original estimate of £2,200,000 for the line had rocketed to £3,800,000, a rather large oversight.

From Settle Junction the line begins an unbroken climb of 1 in 100 to Blea Moor, affectionately known to generations of railwaymen as "The Long Drag". After Settle village the line cuts through the short Stainforth Tunnel (120 yards) where many a northbound steam-hauled special has slipped to a halt with wet leaves on the tracks, especially the light-weight SR WC Class No.34072 *City of Wells* a locomotive which looks distinctly out of place in the Northern Fells. Three miles further on is Horton-in-Ribblesdale, then Selside and eventually Ribblehead Station which is extremely isolated as it lies at 1,025 ft. above sea level. Just beyond the station is the controversial Ribblehead Viaduct with its 24 arches, 104 ft. above ground level. This viaduct has become a thorn in BR's side with estimates to repair the structure being as varied as the predictions of the life span BR gave the structure eight years ago! Blea Moor Tunnel is the next feature on the route which signals the end of the long climb from Settle Junction. The tunnel which took four years to build is 1 mile 869 yards long, and opens out into beautiful Dentdale where the line runs over Denthead (199 yards) and Arten Gill viaducts (220 yards) and on towards Dent station, famous as the highest station in England at 1,145 ft. above sea level. The village of Dent itself is four miles away down the valley. Just after Dent the 1,213 yard Rise Hill Tunnel is met and the line drops down into Garsdale (Hawes Junction until 1st September, 1932); the branch to Hawes can just be made out through the undergrowth opposite the remains of the locomotive turntable once situated here. The branch was run by the North-Eastern Railway and eventually linked up with the ECML at Northallerton.

From Garsdale the line runs across Dandry Mire Viaduct which was originally to have been an embankment, and then starts to climb towards the tunnels at Moorcock (98 yards) and Shotlock Hill (106 yards) after which the highest point of the line at Ais Gill is reached at 1,169 ft. above sea level. The next 15 miles to Ormside are a continual descent at 1 in 100 crossing firstly Ais Gill Viaduct (87 yards) and then running along the ledge of the wild Mallerstang Common with Wild Boar Fell at 2,342 ft. dominating the scene. After Mallerstang is the short Birkett Tunnel (424 yards) which opens out on to the softer Eden Valley landscape. Kirkby Stephen is the next station reached, two miles from the town of the same name, and from here the line crosses the highest viaduct on the route at Smardale, 131 ft. above Scandal Beck and the trackbed remains of the Lancashire and South Durham Union Railway route between Barnard Castle and Tebay, a line closed in 1962. Smardale is the last piece of major engineering work as the route continues along the Eden Valley between Lazonby and Cotehill. The next large station is Appleby, famous for its annual gypsy horse fair, and where the Kirkby Stephen to Penrith line used to converge. Then it is a straight forward journey into Carlisle where the line, running side by side with the Newcastle line at Petteril Bridge Junction, enters the city.

In its heyday the Settle and Carlisle only saw six trains a day in each direction, and with the formation of the London, Midland and Scottish Company in 1923, the rivalry between the Midland and the London and North Western had virtually disappeared, sowing the seeds for a run down of the route. By the 1950's the line saw three day and two night expresses including the famous "Thames Clyde" working, which would eventually be cut back from its St. Pancras departure to Nottingham and then removed from the route altogether at the start of the May 1982 timetable, running instead via the Hope Valley, Manchester, Preston and then the WCML into Glasgow.

The line became infamous during the 1947 and 1963 snow storms. In 1947 the line was blocked for two months and even German prisoners-of-war armed with a giant flame thrower could not remove the compacted snow. In 1963 the Edinburgh to London sleeper was stranded in snow drifts south of Rise Hill Tunnel.

During the early 1960's, when the prototype Deltic was being tested over the route, there was a proposal to withdraw all passenger services and divert them over the WCML route. Since the turn of the Century, annual ticket sales had dropped from 150,000 to only 35,000. However, the Minister of Transport refused the proposal, and in 1964 also decided not to close the intermediate stations between Settle and Appleby on hardship grounds. In fact in 1964 the situation improved with the introduction of DMU's to the line, but this was short-lived and a closure proposal was implemented on the 4th May, 1970. By 1971 all goods service facilities had been withdrawn from stations on the route.

But then a small miracle happened with the transfer of WCML traffic to the route whilst that line was being electrified. Another problem had also surfaced for BR. How could they run slow freight trains on the WCML in a system soon to be used by 100 mph electric trains? The answer of course was simple. Run them over the Settle and Carlisle. So the line was reprieved and in fact became heavily used by freight traffic, some track being relaid and some sections of line receiving colour light signalling!

In 1975 the "Dales Rail" service was introduced and some stations were reopened including, Dent, Garsdale, and Kirkby Stephen West (Kirkby Stephen East, nearer the town of that name, being on the closed Barnard Castle to Tebay line). On the 1st May, 1976 the line celebrated its 100th birthday with many specials over the route to celebrate the occasion no railway enthusiast ever expected to see.

In 1978 limited steam specials were allowed back over the route and this culminated in 1980 with the "Cumbrian Mountain Pullman" trains. The feeling of well-being was to last just 12 months when, in early 1981, BR dropped the 'bombshell' about the structural weakness

Arten Gill Viaduct is crossed by Class 47/4 No.47488 Rail Riders on the 12.42 Carlisle to Leeds working of the 9th September, 1988. In the foreground are abandoned snow fences, and the line can be seen clearly running along the edge of Dent Fell and on towards Dent Station. The 1,825ft. Rise Hill, is prominent in the background.

of Ribblehead Viaduct. A statement at the time that the viaduct had only five years of useful life has proved untrue, but it was obvious the writing was on the wall because in May 1982, BR diverted away the Nottingham to Glasgow trains. The next blow came in May 1983 when the remaining freight traffic was routed away due to the fact that it was now compatible to run block trains on the WCML which, at speeds of up to 80mph, integrated well with express workings.

Motive power on the route has varied over the last 100 years and has included Midland Railway built 4-4-0s from 1877, LMS Compounds, Deeley 999 4-4-0s which were constructed specially for the line, and the more modern types of steam power including Black 5s, Stanier 8Fs, 4Fs, Crabs, Britannia Pacifics, and also LMS Jubilees. With the closure of

Above: Eastfield-based Class 47 No.47644 The Permanent Way Institution leaves the northern portal of the 1 mile 869 yards Blea Moor Tunnel with the 16.33 Leeds to Carlisle train on the 6th June, 1988. Blea Moor which rises above the tunnel has changed considerably in the last twenty years with the planting of a large conifer forest on its northern edge above the tunnel. The repeater signal is so placed because southbound locomotive crews had difficulty in sighting the Blea Moor distant signal. The permanent way hut standing by the repeater signal is still in use.

Below: Visitors to the line on the 30th January, 1988, were Class 50 Nos.50008 and 50034 on the Fellsman Railtour which had run from Swindon up the WCML to Carlisle, returning southwards over the Settle and Carlisle. The train is about to enter Shotlock Hill Tunnel and escape from the driving rain and heavy mist which had descended on the Fells that particular day. Class 50s are no strangers to the Settle and Carlisle route being regular performers in the early 1970's with freight and WCML diversions. Eventually during 1973-74, they were transferred to the Western Region on the completion of electrification between Preston and Glasgow.

Carlisle Kingmoor amd Leeds Holbeck sheds in 1968 and 1967, Class 45 'Peaks' took over the passenger workings including the prestigious "Thames-Clyde Express". In turn, the 'Peaks' gave way to Class 47 power. Freight traffic was usually in the hands of the now withdrawn Classes 25 and 40.

The line itself had no locomotive sheds to call its own on the 72 mile section between Settle Junction and Petteril Bridge Junction, although Hellifield Shed was on the southern fringe of the line. This was quite a large Midland depot and engines from here were sometimes used to bank trains up the 1 in 100 "Long Drag" from Settle Junction. The shed closed in 1963, the year many services became diesel-hauled, but was used to store withdrawn steam engines for a few months before being demolished. The depot for Hawes Junction (Garsdale) never materialised although a turntable was located here to turn engines which had banked from Hellifield. Steam motive power for the line was supplied by two depots, namely, Carlisle Kingmoor and Leeds Holbeck: in later years Holbeck also supplied the 'Peak' motive power. The last remaining Jubilees were shedded here and had their swan song on the Settle and Carlisle in the summer of 1967 when they worked the summer Saturday relief trains through from Leeds. The locos were specially cleaned by a group of enthusiasts who, on a Friday night would descend on Holbeck shed under cover of darkness and spend the entire early hours polishing some pride back into the once prestigious engines, efforts that were not to go unnoticed by the many lineside photographers, not to mention the BR authorities!

Today the line is attracting more passenger traffic than ever with the usual five coach trains being increased to ten. The present timetable sees five trains from the Leeds direction and four from Carlisle on Monday to Saturday, with two each way on Sundays. Most trains are Class 47 hauled but there is a diagram for a two-car 1st generation DMU set which has been recently extended to four cars. Most trains during the summer of 1988 were full to capacity which points to the fact that the line can be run as a commercial proposition.

Class 47/4 No.47479 runs into Garsdale Station over Dandry Mire Viaduct (originally to have been an embankment when the line was surveyed) with the 16.09 Carlisle to Leeds on the 9th September, 1988. To the left of the engine was the site of the turntable located here for steam engines which had banked up from Settle Junction. To the right beyond the buffer stops the Hawes Branch continued to Northallerton. The solitary building in the centre of the picture used to be a chapel for the local community in the railway houses located just behind the viaduct. The distant hill is Great Shunner Fell, 2,349ft. above sea level.

Right: In typical Settle and Carlisle weather of heavy rain and strong winds, Class 47/4 No.47406 (formerly named Rail Riders) enters Dent, at 1,145ft. above sea level, the highest station in England, with the 10.45 Leeds to Carlisle train on the 1st September, 1988. 47406 is the only 'Generator' Class 47 to receive InterCity livery, being painted specially for its naming ceremony which was run as a competition by the BR Rail Riders Club for junior enthusiasts. Rail Riders lost its plates to No.47488 when it was reallocated to secondary duties based at Immingham. It is pleasing to see at least two people boarding the train in view of the appalling weather conditions that day.

Below: Denthead Viaduct, as the name suggests, is located at the head of beautiful yet isolated Dentdale. Class 47/4 No.47401 North Eastern (name since removed) passes with an eight-coach train of Mark 1 stock on the 10.45 Leeds to Carlisle working of the 6th June, 1988. The ten spans of the 197 feet long viaduct blend well with the surrounding moorland. To the right of the picture was Dent Head signal box, closed in 1965 when all the semaphore signals were removed from the area. The hills in the background extend up to Whernside over which the Dales Way path runs.

Trans-Pennine Routes

The Pennine Chain, often referred to as the backbone of England, had for many years presented the railway engineers of this country with a great physical challenge. The counties of Lancashire and Yorkshire, along with County Durham and Westmorland (now part of Cumbria), were in need of suitable rail links to help improve the prosperity they were enjoying by the early 1800's. Lancashire had its cotton trade, whilst Yorkshire relied on its woollen manufacturing. From the east, County Durham wanted to transport coke and coal to the iron ore mines around Barrow, and the ore in return needed to be despatched to the blast furnaces of Teeside.

On an east-west basis, six lines emerged to cross the Pennines.
1. The Stainmore Route
2. The Copy Pit Route
3. The Calder Valley Route
4. The Standedge Route
5. The Woodhead Route
6. The Hope Valley Route

The Stainmore Route

The Parliamentary Act for this line was passed on 13th July, 1857, and gave the go-ahead for the South Durham and Lancashire Union Railway to construct a line between Tebay in the west and Barnard Castle to the east. The first sod was cut by the Duke of Cleveland on 25th August, 1857, at Kirkby Stephen. By early 1860, many of the stone viaducts were completed including Percy Beck, Hatygill, and Merrygill as well as the metal structures at Belah and Deepdale. Also 17 miles of permanent way out of a total of the 34¾ miles had been laid between Tebay and Barnard Castle. The line opened for public passenger services on the 8th August, 1861, following a special ceremony for invited guests the previous day. First services included just two trains each way per day between Tebay and Barnard Castle, a procedure that was to continue for the next ten years. The line was to become profitable with its freight operations: coke and coal being transported westwards to Barrow, and iron ore eastwards to the blast furnaces of Teeside. The superior ore from Barrow could be mixed with the inferior ore from Teeside to produce a first class steel product.

Like all Pennine routes, snow was a continuing hazard during the winter months. In fact some railwaymen reckoned that summer never arrived on the line as they could remember snow at Stainmore Summit in August! Trains were often stuck in drifts for days on end, the longest saga beginning on the 3rd February, 1947. A Kirkby Stephen to Darlington train became stuck in the climb up to the summit. Passengers were rescued and brought back to Kirkby Stephen, but the snow continued to fall and blizzard conditions were encountered. The permanent way gangs worked day and night and even used flame throwers to try and clear the route. The line was eventually reopened at the end of March, a closure of two months!

Gradually freight traffic began to decline while passenger traffic never reached the expected peak, and the line was closed in January 1962, just managing to reach its one hundredth birthday. All tracks have now been lifted but the route is worth exploring by foot, especially between Kirkby Stephen and Barnard Castle. Most of the stone viaducts are intact, but the metal structures at Belah and Deepdale were demolished soon after the line closed, so a diversion is necessary, as well as a great deal of stamina! The signalbox guarding the now non-existent Belah Viaduct still stands 26 years after the demolition gangs left. It is used by the local sheep population as a shelter from the harsh Pennine weather. The stations at Kirkby Stephen, Barras and Bowes still stand, but the station at Barnard Castle was demolished and a factory car park has taken its place.

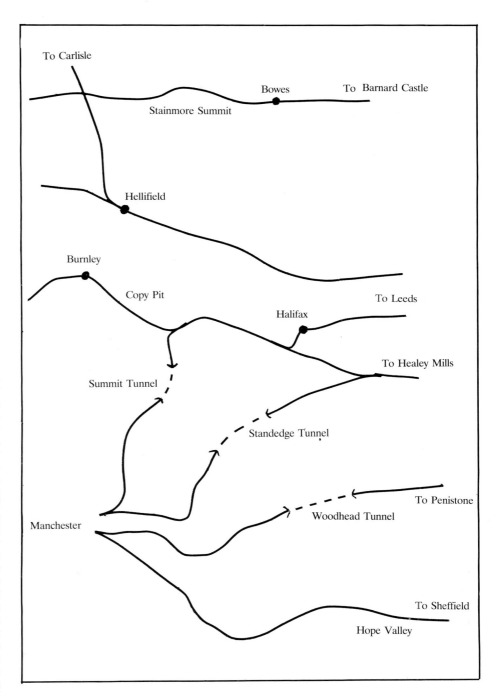

The Copy Pit Route

The effects of an Ice Age glacier which forced its way down from Burnley in the west, through the Cliviger Gorge and out into the Calder Valley in the east, aided the bridging of the Pennines along this rail route. In 1844 the Manchester and Leeds Railway decided to build a branch from their main line at Hall Royd Junction, near Todmorden, over to Burnley to give them a more direct route to Preston and Blackpool. Thomas Gooch was appointed to survey the line and an Act was passed on the 30th June, 1845, the line opening on the 12th November, 1849, by which time the Manchester and Leeds had become part of the Lancashire and Yorkshire Railway. The line was difficult to construct and involved a severe climb to the summit at Copy Pit (749 ft. above sea level). After leaving the main line the branch climbed for 3½ miles at 1 in 65, and 1 in 80 passing through the 290 yard Kitson Wood Tunnel, which opened out onto Nott Wood Viaduct. After the summit the line dropped down to Burnley at a gradient of 1 in 68. In 1866 the original terminus at Burnley Thorneybank was replaced by the present station, namely Manchester Road. The line became primarily a freight route between Lancashire and Yorkshire, and in 1906 loops were installed at Holme and Portsmouth. However, on summer Saturdays the line was popular with excursion trains from industrial Yorkshire to the seaside resort of Blackpool.

During the last days of steam the route attracted many lineside photographers because, with the closure of Carlisle Kingmoor, Rose Grove depot near Burnley became a focal point for steam working over the steeply graded Southern Pennines. Many trains worked from Healey Mills, Wakefield, over the Copy Pit route to Wyre Dock, Fleetwood, usually in the hands of Stanier 8Fs allocated to Rose Grove. During the last few months of these workings, volunteer cleaners were at work again, and the Rose Grove drivers felt obliged to put on the 'black smoke effects' having arrived at the depot in the early hours of the morning to find their 8Fs sporting a Sunday best coat of black paint with red buffer beam to match!

Today the line is devoid of all freight traffic, for it was diverted to other Trans-Pennine routes several years ago. Passengers are conveyed by Pacers and Sprinters operating on the "Roses Link" between Blackpool North and York, set up originally on the initiative of the Burnley and Bradford Building Societies which had merged and needed a reliable form of transport between the two head offices. Occasional football specials use the line and, during 1988, a charter HST special from London travelled the route.

The Calder Valley Route

This line was approved under an Act of Parliament on the 4th July, 1836, and work by the Manchester and Leeds Railway had begun by August 1837, under the direction of the engineer George Stephenson and his assistant Thomas Gooch (elder brother to Daniel of Great Western Railway fame). The line was opened to Littleborough on the 4th July, 1839, with seven trains operating each way between Manchester and Littleborough. Further to the west, Rochdale was a fast growing cotton town. The use of the Rochdale Canal had made the movement of the finished cotton product so much easier. The canal authorities had opposed the coming of the railway because they knew it would render them redundant virtually overnight, something which in fact happened! From Rochdale, the Manchester and Leeds Railway crossed the Pennines by the Littleborough to Todmorden gorge, but a major tunnel, 2,885 yards long, was constructed at Summit. The through-route between Lancashire and Yorkshire opened on the 1st March, 1841, forging a link between Manchester, Rochdale, Leeds and York.

The opening of the line gave Manchester a second route to London which although indirect was taken very seriously by the Grand Junction Railway whose route was via Newton Junction, and Birmingham. The new route by the Manchester and Leeds was via Derby. Both Companies charged the same fares as competition was fierce, neither Company

---

A view from the disused platforms of Bowes station on the erstwhile Stainmore route, showing the new A66 road deviation which has been built over the railway trackbed to ease congestion and heavy lorries from the narrow streets of Bowes village. This Trans-Pennine route was closed in 1962, just managing to celebrate its 100th birthday. At Stainmore Summit itself the A66 route has been widened into a dual carriageway, again utilizing the former trackbed.

wanting to lose their own customers. The Grand Junction route was, of course, always to be the quicker of the two. The Manchester and Leeds also introduced the first 'paste board' tickets which could be date-stamped, a system designed by Thomas Edmondson of Lancaster. This method of issuing tickets was later adopted by the whole of the railway network.

Today the line sees Sprinter DMU workings between Manchester, Rochdale, Halifax, Bradford and Leeds. There are 22 workings each way Monday to Saturday and 13 on Sundays. The Summit route caters for a great deal of freight traffic and includes Fidlers Ferry to Healey Mills traffic, Stanlow Oil Refinery to Leeds and Jarrow, Weaste (Manchester) to Port Clarence and Glazebrook to the Humber Oil Refinery. The Summit tunnel had to be closed in December 1984, after a petrol tanker train from Haverton Hill to Glazebrook caught fire after being derailed in the tunnel. The BR crew of driver and guard managed to un-couple the first three tanks and draw them out of the tunnel, thus saving the engine from certain destruction. The fire burned for two days, and the tunnel had to be left for seven days to cool down. It then took three months for the wreckage to be removed and cut up. The tunnel did not collapse as had been feared, a great credit to the Victorian engineers. After the inside had been relined at a cost of £1 million, the tunnel reopened again for traffic on the 19th August, 1985, the first train through being the 06.20 Leeds to Manchester Victoria.

The Standedge Route

It was the Huddersfield Canal Company which stirred the Manchester and Leeds Railway into building this particular line across the Pennines between Stalybridge and Huddersfield. In 1811 the Canal Company had opened its own route through the Pennines, having constructed the longest canal tunnel in Britain at Standedge. By 1845 it had formed itself into a railway and canal company and was proposing to build a line from the Manchester and Leeds Railway at Cooper Bridge to the Sheffield, Ashton-under-Lyne and Manchester Railway at Stalybridge. By the 1st August, 1849, the Huddersfield and Leeds line had been built, and various companies including the Leeds, Dewsbury and Manchester, along with the Manchester and Leeds, had been incorporated into the LNWR, which built the line under Standedge. When the route opened, Standedge tunnel between Diggle in Lancashire and Marsden in Yorkshire became the longest tunnel on the railway network of the time, being 3 miles 66 yards in length, although at this point it was still a single bore.

The nearby canal, originally belonging to the Huddersfield Canal Company, became extremely important during the construction of the railway tunnel, because it was used to carry materials to and from the site. A second single bore was opened in February 1871, and in August 1894, a double bore was opened, thus giving four tracks between Lancashire and Yorkshire. As traffic declined in the early 1960's, the two single tunnels were closed and the ventilation shafts sealed.

Today this Pennine crossing is probably the busiest passenger route of all. The line sees the important Liverpool to Newcastle workings still loco-hauled by Class 47s in 1989, but shortly to be in the hands of Class 158 Express Units. The Liverpool to Newcastle trains have employed various forms of diesel traction enjoying a final fling on BR before being destined for the scrap yard. These have included Deltics and, recently, Peaks. When the Deltics were ousted from the crack ECML express turns, they were transferred away from Finsbury Park and Haymarket depots to York from where they were regularly used on Liverpool to Newcastle diagrams until they were finally withdrawn in 1981. Thereafter, the Peaks took over and gave sterling service until the start of the May, 1987 timetable when a select band of Class 47s (the early "generator" series Nos.47401-420) were employed on the turns, allocated to Gateshead. These eventually gave way to a Provincial Sector allocation of Class 47s based at Crewe, because of the closure of Gateshead depot in early 1988. Minor exams can be carried out on these locos at Allerton Depot in Liverpool, but any major work is undertaken at Crewe. No.47401, the pioneer of the class and originally numbered D1500 has recently lost its "North Eastern" nameplates to 47443 (now Crewe-based with North Eastern plates!), and in fact all the remaining "generators" have lost their names and have been relegated to secondary duties working out of Immingham.

Daytime freight working over Standedge is relatively rare because of the numerous passenger diagrams, but two block oil trains are booked from Glazebrook to Haverton Hill. More traffic operates during the night when the line is quieter, and these can include Folly Lane (Runcorn), to Grimsby traffic as well as Holyhead to Humber Oil Refinery, Walton Old Junction to Haverton Hill, Seal Sands to Folly Lane, and Lindsey Oil Refinery to Oakleigh. Some of these workings are Class 56 hauled, a class rarely seen in this part of the country but, in the main, locomotives are of Classes 37 and 47.

The remains of Bowes Station closed in 1961. The station land has been purchased by a local farmer and part of the station yard has been built over. How long will it be before there is no trace of this former Trans-Pennine line in this isolated location?

The Woodhead Route

The Sheffield, Ashton-under-Lyne and Manchester Railway was incorporated by an Act of Parliament in May, 1837, the first sod being cut on the 1st October, 1838, and the first section opened from Manchester, Travis St. to Godley on 17th November, 1841. From May, 1842, the line shared the Manchester, London Road terminus, (now Piccadilly) with the London and Birmingham Railway, and services were extended to Broadbottom. By August, 1844, the line had reached Woodhead where the tunnel had been under construction since September, 1839. When opened on 22nd December, 1845, it was 3 miles and 22 yards in length. A parallel bore was opened on the 2nd February, 1852, completing a double line throughout, although in single bores.

The cost in both lives and money was high. Thirty-two navvies were killed during the construction of the first tunnel, and the financial bill finally came to three times the original estimate. 273,000 tons of spoil was removed, helped along by 157 tons of gunpowder. During the building of the second bore tragedy struck in the form of a cholera epidemic, and 29 people perished, including two nurses. All are buried in the churchyard at Woodhead.

Provision for a double track tunnel was first considered in 1882, but the scheme was promptly dropped for financial reasons. But many years later in 1945, when the two original single bore tunnels were in desperate need of repair, the scheme was reintroduced. In 1948 a contract was placed to build the new Woodhead Tunnel, to be ready for use with the new 1500v dc electric locomotives which were being built at Gorton in Manchester. Work began on the tunnel in 1949 and was completed by 1953, the first electric train running on the 3rd June. The new tunnel cost £4¼ million and with health and safety checks being carried out more frequently in the 1950's the death toll was reduced to six. In 1963 the two closed single bore tunnels were brought back into use again by the Electricity Board which laid electric cables through the tunnels linking Stalybridge with Doncaster. Many people had objected to unsightly pylons which would have straddled the moors above the tunnels.

The Woodhead route was to become the most modern line in Britain by the time it had been electrified in 1954. The idea of electrification had been approved in 1936 but with the coming of World War 2, work was shelved and did not start until 1947, the electrification being completed in three stages. Wath to Dunford Bridge was commissioned in 1952, Manchester to Dunford Bridge in June, 1954, and Sheffield to Penistone in September, 1954. Work also began on building the 58 Bo-Bo mixed traffic engines and 7 Co-Co express locomotives. After construction they were maintained at two depots, Reddish in the west and Wath in the east.

However, after the initial surge of traffic during the late fifties, the first nail in the route's coffin had been hammered home by the withdrawal of all through-traffic between London Marylebone and Manchester over the Woodhead line. A Sheffield to Manchester Piccadilly local service was substituted instead, but by 1965 many of these trains had been diverted to the Hope Valley route. By 1970 the line was freight only with around 60 block trains a day consisting mainly of coal, sand, steel and chemicals. To match the freight needs, thirty of the Bo-Bos had been converted to work in multiple. A reduction in wagon loads by 1979 saw the closure of most yards along the route, and during the next two years traffic became increasingly rare. The axe finally fell on the 20th July, 1981, when the route was closed between Hadfield in the west and Penistone in the east, leaving only local services at each end. The final train to traverse the route was the 20.53 Harwich, Parkestone Quay, to Liverpool Speedlink service on the 18th July, 1981. On the 10th December, 1984, the remaining overhead 1500dc wires from Manchester to Glossop and Hadfield were re-energised at 25kv to fit in with the rest of the BR system. These local services are well patronised by local commuters, and trains run at 15 minute intervals at peak times and 30 minutes during off-peak hours. The EMUs which operate these services are of Classes 303 and 304 variety, the former running in the Greater Manchester Transport Authority livery, the latter in BR corporate blue and grey.

Although the heart of this famous route has been ripped out, the arteries left on the west side of the Pennines are still beating strongly.

Left: Pacer unit No.142089 passes over Nott Wood Viaduct after leaving the 290 yard long Kitson Wood Tunnel on its climb up to the Copy Pit summit on the Burnley to Todmorden Trans-Pennine route. The train is the 13.51 York to Preston and is one of only 11 passenger services which now use this line; a far cry from the days when Stanier 8Fs used to struggle up the gradients with Healey Mills to Fleetwood (Wyre Dock) trains. Today the line is completely devoid of freight traffic, it having all been diverted away to other Trans-Pennine routes a few years ago.

Below: In beautiful Pennine scenery Sprinter Unit No.150237 and Pacer Unit 142088 form the 09.49 York to Blackpool North working, pictured on the 1 in 80 climb up to Copy Pit summit on 6th August, 1988. The Pacer train is the Castleford to Blackpool which runs on Summer Saturdays only and links up with the York portion of the train at Bradford Interchange.

The Hope Valley Route

Ways of connecting Manchester with Sheffield were being discussed as early as 1820, and by 1830 the Sheffield and Manchester Railway had issued a prospectus stating its intentions of linking up with the Liverpool and Manchester Railway. This was to be a difficult route to construct because the line would have to cut through the North Derbyshire Peak District and, in fact, two tunnels had to be cut, one being Cowburn (2 miles 182 yards) at the Chinley end, the other Totley Tunnel (3 miles 950 yards) on the Sheffield side. Totley was to become the second longest tunnel on BR, whilst Cowburn became the ninth.

George Stephenson, who had been appointed engineer for the line, proposed a rather difficult and inadequate route which would have involved severe line gradients, with the route reaching a summit some 1,000 ft. above each terminus. By 1833 the shareholders were given their money back and the route was abandoned, traffic going by the Woodhead route until the 1890's.

In 1884 the Dore and Chinley Railway decided to build an alternative route via the Hope Valley which would include less severe gradients than George Stephenson's proposed route. The Midland became interested in this line because it would link the company's lines at each end, and by 1888 the Midland had taken over the building of the line, employing engineers who had helped construct the Settle and Carlisle route.

Whilst the line was being built it was denounced by one, John Ruskin, who was concerned that the Industrial Revolution had ruined the environment, and the thought of the railway running through Edale infuriated him. In fact the coming of the line stopped the drift of population from Edale and brought about residential development within the area. The line was eventually opened to goods on the 6th November, 1893, and to regular passenger traffic on the 1st June, 1894, thus completing another Pennine crossing.

When the electrified Woodhead route closed in 1981, a great deal of extra traffic in the form of freight was brought to the line, but this has since decreased and regular freight workings now comprise only cement trains from the Blue Circle complex at Hope. During the 1970's the line carried nineteen through trains a day including two to St.Pancras using the Dore South Curve. It also saw nine stopping trains.

In May 1982, the Nottingham to Glasgow and Edinburgh trains were diverted over the Hope Valley route away from the Settle and Carlisle line, creating new connections for these services from Sheffield for Doncaster, Grimsby and Cleethorpes. The line in recent years has also seen three named trains running over the route from Harwich. "The European" ran to Glasgow and Edinburgh, "The Rhinelander" to Manchester Piccadilly maintaining a long tradition of rail connections between the two centres, and "The Loreley" which runs as a two-car Class 156 Sprinter unit destined for Blackpool North. The latter is a far cry from the days when "The European" and "The Rhinelander" were loco-hauled and consisted of ten coaches with buffet facilities. Not surprisingly, BR have encountered overcrowding on these two car Sprinters, and are hoping to increase them to four in the near future.

Freight on the line is restricted to the workings from the Blue Circle Cement works at Hope which has numerous sidings and despatches block trains to Widnes, Pean Forest, Northenden and Dewsbury. Coal also arrives at Hope in the form of three merry-go-round workings per week from Healey Mills. Through freight workings are restricted to a Worksop to Warrington Arpley Speedlink duty.

Below: **Class 47/0 No.47190 Pectinidae**, in new Railfreight Petroleum subsector livery, applied by RFS Industries of Hull — the first time BR diesels have been painted by private contractors — powers an additional Leeds-Stanlow oil empties towards Littleborough on the Calder Valley Trans-Pennine route. The train has just left Summit Tunnel. This was the tunnel closed for six months in 1985 when a chemical working became derailed in the tunnel and caught fire, the repair bill for reconstruction of the tunnel eventually topping £1 million. The picture was taken on the 12th December, 1988.

Above: Approaching Diggle Tunnel (3 miles 66 yards) on the Standedge route is Class 37/5 No.37503 with the 6E20 Glazebrook to Haverton Hill oil tanks on a snowy and stormy day in February 1988. The Diggle route sees little freight work for the majority of workings use the Calder Valley line. The mast on the hill top is a booster station for radio and TV signals.

Below: Literally the end of the line at Hadfield on the erstwhile Woodhead electrified Trans-Pennine route. The sign tells electric train drivers to STOP HERE. They could not go much further if they tried! The overhead cables have been converted to the standard 25kv and a busy commuter service runs from here into Manchester Piccadilly.
In 1954 when the line was electrified, it became the most modern railway route in the country, but during the late 60's traffic declined and the through services between Marylebone and Manchester via Sheffield were withdrawn. By 1970, the line was carrying freight only, and did so until the final day came in July 1981, when all remaining freight traffic was transferred to other Pennine routes.

Above: Class 47/4 No.47413, one of the original 'Generator' Class 47s is pictured by Diggle Junction signal box on the 12.15 Newcastle to Liverpool Lime Street on the 12th February, 1988. The land to the right used to contain numerous busy sidings, a legacy of the time when Diggle could boast two single and one double bore tunnel. Today the single bores are sealed and only the double tunnel remains in use. The signal box was known as Diggle Junction because it was here the parallel line from Stalybridge via Micklehurst and Uppermill diverged, thus making it a junction with the main line between Lancashire and Yorkshire.

Below: Class 47/4 No.47407 Aycliffe passes beneath the snow-topped Pots and Pans Hill, Greenfield, with the 08.25 Newcastle to Liverpool Lime Street working during February, 1988. Local legend has it that a fatal duel between two giants took place here, the legacy of which is the boulder-strewn hillside. The truth, of course, is that Ice Age glaciers were the real culprits, depositing large rocks called erratics, when the ice melted.

The Peak Forest

By 1863 the Midland Railway had reached Buxton on its push north from St.Pancras, but here it was to find its route into Manchester blocked by the LNWR, which ran a line from Buxton via Whaley Bridge and Stockport into central Manchester. The powers that be decided to build a line from Blackwell Mill Junction, Millers Dale, to the Peak Forest, through Dove Holes Tunnel (1 mile 1224 yards) to meet up with the Manchester, Sheffield and Lincolnshire Railway at New Mills. This line opened in 1865, through trains to Manchester, London Road, beginning on the 1st February, 1867. By 1880 Midland services were running into Manchester Central via Stockport and the joint connection from Romiley to Bredbury Junction. However, the Midland still found that journey times over this route were very slow and decided to build a cut off from south of New Mills through Disley Tunnel to Heaton Mersey, a line which opened throughout to goods on the 4th May, 1902, to passengers on the 1st July. This now gave the Midland a fast run into the heart of

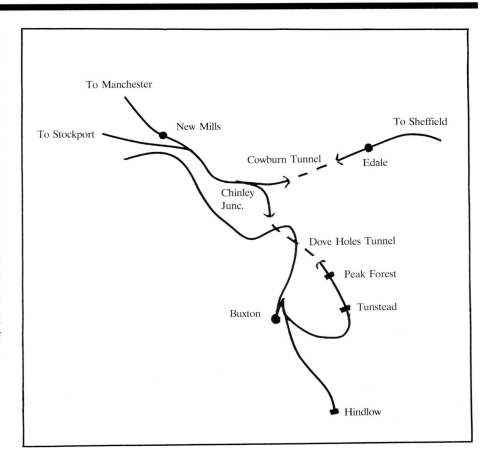

Class 47/3 No.47356 rounds the curve at Chinley South Junction as it takes the Hope Valley route to Sheffield with the 7A22 Peak Forest to Bletchley limestone working of the 25th March, 1988. The wagons are of the MSV type and are 30 years old. The Peakstone Company have had their own modern fleet of limestone wagons built, and they lease them to BR. Eventually all MSV wagons will be phased out. In the background is Harpur Hill, 1662ft. above sea level.

Manchester and enabled it to compete with the Great Central services. Central Station became a very busy terminus, with over 400 trains arriving and departing each day.

During the electrification of the ex-LNWR main line from Euston to Manchester Piccadilly in the 1960's, all London traffic was diverted over the Midland line via the Peak Forest and Derby to St.Pancras. However, completion of the electrification meant the death sentence for the Midland route between Chinley and Matlock as a major passenger carrying line. On the 6th March, 1967, all local Manchester Central to Derby stopping trains were withdrawn with complete closure of the Romiley to Bredbury Junction link. Buxton Midland station was also closed on the same day. Expresses from St.Pancras and Derby into Manchester Central followed this route until the 1st January, 1968 when they were transferred to run via Chesterfield and into Manchester Piccadilly. The ex-Midland route between Matlock and Peak Forest was closed and lifted.

By 1968 all freight traffic was being handled by the few remaining Stanier 8Fs based at Buxton, the shed serving the needs of the numerous local quarries and limestone works. Whichever route these sturdy freight engines worked, climbing was the order of the day, with gradients of 1 in 90 through Dove Holes Tunnel and equally demanding work was required for the climb out of Great Rocks Dale. Steam came to an end over the Manchester to Derby route with the closure of Buxton shed on the 4th March, 1968, when the surviving freight-hauled trains were handed over to diesels. Express passenger workings by this time were being performed by the Class 45 'Peaks', but four months later in July, 1968, these services were diverted away via Chesterfield leaving the line between Chinley and Peak Forest freight only.

Today the area around Buxton and the Peak Forest is still rich in natural limestone, a feature which provides BR Railfreight sector with a great deal of revenue, and has also meant the 'survival' of the famous ex-Midland route to London between Chinley and Peak Forest Junction. Passenger diversions are rare over this stretch of line, but on February 14th, 1988, engineering work between Chinley North Junction and Hazel Grove overran, and the Sheffield to Liverpool local workings, then in the hands of Class 31/4s, were diverted over the freight only route. This was much to the delight of local enthusiasts, but a headache for the local BR management team who were rather hard pressed to fit in the local Manchester Piccadilly to Buxton trains with the diverted Sheffield trains, as well as the freight traffic that was also running that day! The signalman at Buxton must surely have earned his double pay!

There are two quarries in the Buxton area, at Dove Holes and Tunstead, which despatch vast quantities of limestone by train to destinations throughout the country. The ex-Midland line between Chinley and Peak Forest Junction was retained solely to service these important freight workings, and also to keep a large number of lorries off the narrow roads in the Peak Forest area. The line is double tracked between Chinley South Junction and Great Rocks Junction, but has been singled between Great Rocks and Buxton.

The quarry at Tunstead is the largest limestone complex outside the USA, and currently 4 million tonnes are mined each year. The quarry, which is owned by ICI, has its own shunting locomotives. Also based there are BR staff involved with the TOPS side of the operation. 800,000 tonnes of limestone from Tunstead are despatched annually to the ICI complexes at Northwich and Oakleigh.

Besides the Tunstead-Northwich-Oakleigh workings, block trains also operate to the nearby ICI plant at Hindlow (on the truncated Ashbourne line south of Buxton, closed to passenger services on the 1st November, 1954). The other quarry at Dove Holes is situated just north of the BR sidings at Peak Forest and is operated by Peakstone, but is smaller than the Tunstead operation. Traffic from this quarry is nearly all roadstone and is sent to both Leeds (Balm Road) and Bletchley.

Recently Class 37/5 locomotives have taken over all stone workings, being outstabled at

On the 12th February, 1988, refurbished Class 37/5 Nos.37677 and 37681 double head the heavy 6J46 limestone train out of Peak Forest to Hope Street (Salford) whilst out of the picture, unrefurbished Class 37/0 No.37259 helps by banking. The ICI limestone complex at Tunstead, which despatches thousands of tonnes by rail each year, can be seen in the background, whilst the Peak Forest signal box which controls semaphores on this freight-only line looping round via Buxton, can be noted to the right of the picture. The Class 37/5s which are outstabled at Buxton from Tinsley were converted at Crewe Works, where their main generator was replaced by an alternator, all other mechanical details being the same as the Class 37/0s.

uxton from Tinsley Depot, Sheffield. A and exams are carried out at Buxton depot but ny major work is done at Tinsley. The Class 7/5s usually work in pairs, and at the present me there are five regular diagrams for five airs of engines, leaving three locomotives vailable for maintenance. Locos presently llocated to these services are 37676–688. At e time of writing 37380 of the Class 37/3 ariety is allocated duties at Dove Holes idings both for banking trains out of unstead and for general shunting duties at ove Holes. Some Class 47 power is used ainly on workings to Bletchley and Leeds as ell as Margam and Oakleigh.

One notable point of interest is the ombined use of Tarmac and Peakstone agons on the same working. This involves eakstone wagons being detached at Salford Hope Street) and the train working on to the Tarmac plant in Widnes, the same operation being worked in the reverse direction. This working is affectionately referred to by train crews as the "Big Train" and one can see why as it transports 38 wagons for the two private companies. Major stone workings in the Peak Forest and Buxton area include:

Peak Forest-Washwood Heath
Tunstead-Oakleigh
Peak Forest-Leeds, Balm Road
Peak Forest-Salford, Hope Street
Tunstead-Margam

It is exciting to see that 21 years after closure of the Midland route from St. Pancras to Manchester through the Derbyshire Peak District, a small section of track should still remain, bringing in much needed revenue to the Freight Sector of BR.

Rounding the curve on the approach to Buxworth cutting is Class 47/3 No.47348 St.Christopher's Railway Home which is in Railfreight livery with Peakstone hoppers on the Hope Street (Manchester) to Peak Forest working of the 13th May, 1988. The line used to be quadrupled here on the climb up from Chinley Station to Chinley signalbox, but has been rationalised in recent years because modern diesel traction working heavy freights can easily be integrated into the passenger workings within this area.

Left: Class 31/4 No.31439 climbs up the gradient past Chinley Junction signal box with the 10.45 Liverpool Lime Street to Sheffield on the 25th March, 1988. These services are now in the hands of Class 156 Super Sprinters which work an extended service between Blackpool North and East Anglian destinations, the Class 31s having succumbed at the start of the May 1988 timetable after a reign of just three years on these services. The line in the left foreground is the old Midland main line to St. Pancras via the Peak Forest and Derby, used today for freight-only workings which serve the limestone quarries in the Buxton area.

Above: Running through what could be mistaken for a lunar landscape is Class 37/0 No.37259 complete with snowploughs. The actual location is Peak Forest near Buxton, and the locomotive was shunting loaded limestone wagons to form the 6J46 to Hope Street, Manchester. At the time, 37259 was outstabled at Peak Forest to help with shunting duties and also to bank trains out from the limestone works at Tunstead. To the left of the picture the double track was originally the Midland main line between Manchester Central and St.Pancras via Derby but nowadays is freight only, and has been retained especially for the limestone traffic which emanates from Dove Holes and Tunstead quarries. The locomotive has since been renumbered 37380.

Below: The Permanent Way Engineers seem completely unaware of the passing of refurbished Class 37/5 Nos.37680 and 37679 at New Mills South Junction on the 7H18 Dean Lane (Manchester) to Tunstead limestone empties on the 13th May, 1988. The line by the Midland Railway signal box approaches Manchester through Disley Tunnel and Stockport whilst the track the 37s are occupying reaches Manchester via Marple and Reddish.

Just a trace of black exhaust smoke can be seen as Class 47/0 No.47218 starts the 7T82 from Peak Forest after arriving with the local trip from ICI Hindlow (Briggs Sidings). The working which consists of limestone hoppers is bound for Mossend via Warrington Speedlink Yard. The buildings on the right are the remains of Peak Forest station which was situated on the ex-Midland route from Manchester, and closed in 1968. The route was severed in 1969 and is freight only today. However, the station building remains in use as a mess room and signing-on point for BR train crews.